NEW WAVE

—3—

MARCIA FISK ONG
ROBERT MAPLE

Longman

Contents

Meet some new people

All of these people plan to attend the World Health and Fitness Summer
Institute in Montreal, Canada. Listen to the conversations and guess who is
talking in each of them. Match the number of each conversation to the correct
picture.

Heather Spinelli   Jean Spinelli

Diane Hayworth   Marta Cardoso

Kenji Omura

Yves Remy

Tex Travis

First unit   Looking for a roommate?

0 ⇄
Warm-up

Talk to your classmates about the people they live with.

- Do they live with their parents, with their children, or with a friend?
- Do they have their own bedrooms or do they share a room with someone else?
- Are there any "rules" about noise, neatness, phone calls, etc.?

1 📼
Get ready

Marta Cardoso and Diane Hayworth run into each other one afternoon in downtown Montreal. Listen to Part 1 of their conversation. Then answer these three questions:

1 Where did Marta and Diane meet the first time? *in the Registrationre*
2 Where are both women staying right now? *in a Hotel*
3 What do they hope that somebody is looking for?
   they are looking for a roomate.

2

Dialogue: Part Two

There is an information error in each sentence. Correct it after you listen to Part 2 of the dialogue.

1 Marta wants to rent an apartment. _room_
2 Jean's renting the rooms for a year. _month_
3 Jean's busy at the moment.
4 Jean is Heather's daughter. _mother_
5 Jean's apartment is far from McGill University. _near_
6 Diane quit smoking because of her health. _she want the room._

3

Focus on new language

Find a word or expression in the dialogue with the same meaning.

Words
1 to telephone _call_
2 a person you live with, but who is not a relative _roommate_
3 in fact _actually_
4 children _kids_
5 to stop (doing something) _quit_

Expressions
6 a more formal way of asking permission than "Can I . . . ?" _may I_
7 to have a friendly relationship _get along fine_
8 a brief period of time _a little while_

Two females looking for two others to share four-bedroom apartment for the month of August. Nice neighborhood. Rent is $200 a month (each). Quiet, non-smokers only. Call Jean at 356-2448 between 9 and 6.

Jean: Hello?
Marta: May I speak to Jean, please?
J: Speaking.
M: Hi, my name's Marta Cardoso. I'm calling about your notice for two roommates. Are you still looking for somebody?
J: Yes, I am. But do you want both rooms for yourself?
M: No, I don't. The other one's for a friend of mine, Diane Hayworth.
J: Oh, I see. You understand that I'm renting these rooms just for this month, don't you?
M: Uh-huh. Actually, that's perfect for us. We're attending the World Health and Fitness Summer Institute.
J: Great. I'm here for the Institute too.
M: Oh, I see. Could we see the rooms today?

J: Sure. I'm not doing anything right now. Come on over. By the way, I hope you like kids. The other female is my twelve-year-old daughter, Heather.
M: Oh, I'm sure we'll get along fine. Tell me, where do you live?
J: At 460 University Street, Apartment 1208. It's near McGill University. Do you know where that is?
M: Yes, I do. See you in a little while.

M: I just thought of something, Diane, Jean's notice said "Non-smokers only." What are you going to do?
Diane: So who smokes? I don't.
M: Oh, really? When did you quit?
D: About ten seconds ago! Come on. Let's go and meet Jean!

4 🔲

Focus on pronunciation

Look at these questions. Which syllable has the most stress (emphasis)? Underline it.
Then listen to the tape and confirm your guesses.

1 What's your <u>name</u>?
2 How do you <u>spell</u> your first <u>name</u>?
3 What <u>country</u> are you from?
4 What's your <u>address</u>?
5 What's your <u>phone</u> number?

6 How <u>old</u> are you?
7 What size <u>T-shirt</u> do you wear?
8 How many <u>hours</u> can you work?
9 What days can you <u>help</u>?
10 What time are you <u>free</u>?

11 Do you speak any foreign
    <u>languages</u>?
12 Can you <u>type</u>?
13 Do you know how to <u>drive</u>?
14 Why are you <u>volunteering</u>?

▶ Now rewind the tape and repeat each question.

5 🔁

First practice

Imagine that you are one of the
organizers of the World Health and
Fitness Summer Institute, and you are
looking for several volunteers to act as
translators, guides, etc. Volunteers get
free T-shirts with WHF written
on them. Interview several classmates
and ask appropriate questions for
each blank on the information sheet.
Do not write on the form, so that you
can interview more than one person.

World Health and Fitness Summer Institute

Volunteer Information Sheet

Name: _____

  (last)   *(first)*

Nationality: _____

Address _____

                                  (city)

  _____

  (state/province)   *(zip code)*

Telephone number _____**Age** _____

T-shirt size ____

• **hours you can help a week** _____

• **What days?**_____

• **What time? From**_____**to**_____

• **Foreign languages?** _____
  Which? _____

• **Type?** _____

• **Drive a car?** _____

• **Reasons for volunteering?**

  _____

  _____

  _____

  _____

6
Find the rule

W Question word	Be Form of "Be"	S Subject	(O) ? (Other words)
Who How Why	are was were	you lunch they	? ? late?

W Question word	A Auxiliary verb	S Subject	V Main verb	(O) ? (Other words)
How Where Why	do can are	you we you	like go doing	it ? ? that?

W Question word – the subject	(A) (Auxiliary verb)	V Main verb	(O) ? (Other words)
Who is What (here is the subject) Who	 is	smokes happened calling	? yesterday? ?

(handwritten in margin: no subject!)

▶ Which formula do we use if the question word is also the subject?
  a) W-Be-S? b) W-A-S-V? c) W-(A)-V? *(c circled)*

▶ Which formula do we use if the only verb in the sentence is **am, is, are, was** or **were**?
  a) W-Be-S? b) W-A-S-V? c) W-(A)-V? *(a circled)*

▶ Which formula do we use if there is an auxiliary verb and a main verb?
  a) W-Be-S? b) W-A-S-V? c) W-(A)-V? *(b circled)*

Now apply the rule!

Write the right formula for each question.

1 Where do you live? *WASV ?*
2 Who's that? *WAV ?*
3 Why are they leaving? *WASV?*
4 Who did it? *WAV*
5 How are you feeling now? *WASV*
6 What's happening? *WAV*
7 Where were you yesterday? *W Be S O ?*
8 When can I see you again? *WASVO ?*

7
Transfer

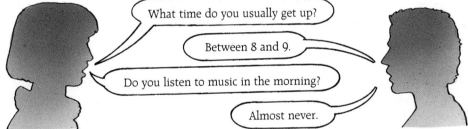

> What time do you usually get up?
>
> Between 8 and 9.
>
> Do you listen to music in the morning?
>
> Almost never.

Student B: Go to page 9.

Student A: Imagine that you and Student B are thinking about sharing an apartment. But first you want to know if you'd be compatible roommates. Are B's habits a problem for you? Ask Student B the following questions. Write O.K. for each answer that is no problem. Find out:

1 What time B usually gets up in the morning.
2 If B listens to music in the morning.
3 What kind of music B prefers.
4 How many hours a day B watches TV.
5 How many nights a week B goes out.
6 How long B stays in the bathroom in the morning.
7 What time B goes to bed on weekends.
8 If B can sleep when there's noise in the apartment.
9 Where B was last Saturday night.
10 If B can cook.

▶ Now answer B's questions. Choose one of these answers, circle it and read it aloud.

11 a) Less than a pack b) More than a pack.
   c) I'm a non-smoker.
12 a) Never. b) Not very often. c) Pretty often.
13 a) Yes, of course. b) Well, almost.
   c) No, I didn't.
14 a) A family member. b) The maid.
   c) I do them myself.
15 a) No, never. b) Not very often.
   c) Very often.
16 a) A few minutes. b) Less than half an hour.
   c) More than half an hour.
17 a) Nobody did. b) One or two people.
   c) More than two people.
18 a) Very rarely. b) Maybe once a week.
   c) More than once a week.
19 a) No, I don't. b) I try to.
   c) I almost always do.
20 a) Most of them do. b) Some of them do.
   c) No, are you kidding?

World Health and Fitness Summer Institute

McGill University, Montreal — August 1–31

Partial list of course offerings

A **Medical Law** (Dr. Jeckle)   M/W/F   2:00 P.M.
Avoid seeing your patients later . . . in court.

B **Macrobiotic Diets**   Tu/Th   8:30 A.M.
Natural foods taste great and they help you live longer.

C **Reducing Stress**   M/W/F   10:00 A.M.
Your life-style might be the reason you're not feeling your best.

D **Eating Disorders**   M/W/F   3:00 P.M.
Treating people who forget to eat or can't stop thinking of eating.

E **Weight Maintenance**   M/W/F   11:00 A.M.
How to combine diet, exercise and life-style to create a new you.

F **Preventing Leg and Foot Injuries**   Tu/Th   1:30 P.M.
Don't let injuries keep you out of the competition.

G **The Organization of a Triathlon**   Tu/Th   10:00 A.M.
How to plan for hundreds of triathletes running, cycling and swimming.

H **You CAN Stop Smoking** (Mr. Camel) M/Tu/W/Th/F   9:00 A.M.
A ten-day program to make you a non-smoker, if you really want to be.

I **Training Course for Life Guards**   M/T/Th/F   12 Noon
If you can swim well, have good eyes and are athletic, a good course.

J **Fast Food or Junk Food?** (Dr. McDonald)   Tu/Th   3:00 P.M.
Is it all the same? Seminar on how to tell the difference.

K **Plastic Surgery: To Have or Not to Have?**   Tu/Th   5:00 P.M.
Want a new face or body? Should you consider plastic surgery?

L **Weight Lifting** (Mr. Schwarzenegger)   M/W/F   5:00 P.M.
Muscle building through basic weight training exercises, with and without weight machines.

M **Run for Your Life** (Ms. Mota)   M/W/F   4:00 P.M.
A reasonable approach to becoming a good jogger.

N **Jazz Dance** (Mr. Davolta)   M/W/F   2:00 P.M.
Dance your way to a better figure and stronger muscles.

O **Avoiding the Common Cold**   Tu/Th   10:00 A.M.
Are colds part of our nature? Can lots of vitamins help?

P **Children and TV Food Commercials**   Tu/Th   1:30 P.M.
Training children to protect themselves from being sold on empty calories.

Q **Daily Exercise Programs**
Sign up for the one that fits your needs.
- **Q1** *Students 9–10 A.M.*
- **Q2** *Young adults 10–11 A.M.*
- **Q3** *Middle agers (40–50) 11 A.M.–12 Noon*
- **Q4** *The Young at Heart (over 50) 3–4 P.M.*
- **Q5** *Busy Executives 12–1 P.M.*
- **Q6** *Overweight People 1–2 P.M.*
- **Q7** *Pregnant Women 2–3 P.M.*
- **Q8** *Professional Athletes 4–6 P.M.*

Read on your own

8 ⇄
Warm-up

Some courses are excellent, many are so-so, and others are actually terrible. Why are some classes better than others? What makes a class "good"?

Work in small groups, and make a list of the five most important characteristics of a good course. Then compare your lists, and try to agree on three main characteristics.

- Teacher always well-prepared?
- Appropriate textbooks?
- Relevant to students?
- Variety of activities in every class?
- Friendly atmosphere?
- Up-to-date material?
- Teacher has high standards?
- Everyone shares ideas?

9
Specific information.

Look at the program for the World Health and Fitness Summer Institute, and find the answers.

1 What time does the course on triathlons meet?
2 Who's teaching the course on jogging?
3 What course meets at 3:00 p.m. on Mondays, Wednesdays and Fridays?
4 Which course can help you to become more muscular?
5 Who teaches the course on the legal aspects of medicine?
6 What time is the daily exercise program for people in their 50's?
7 How long does the non-smokers course last?

10
Focus on words

Look at these two sentences.
Rosa's a good *athlete*.
She's very *athletic*.

▶ Which word is the noun, *athlete* or *athletic*? Which word is the adjective?
▶ Complete the tables with nouns and adjectives you find in the course listings.

Nouns	Adjectives
healt	healthy
part	*partial*
medicine	*medical*
nature	*natural*

Nouns	Adjectives
stress	stressful
	different
reason	
profession	

11 ⇄
Transfer

Discuss which course(s) would be most appropriate for you and your partner.

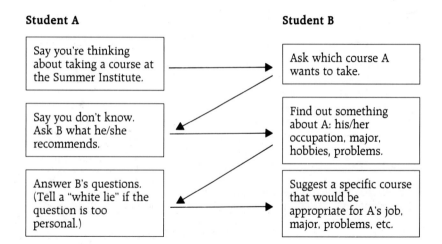

Student A

| Say you're thinking about taking a course at the Summer Institute. |

| Say you don't know. Ask B what he/she recommends. |

| Answer B's questions. (Tell a "white lie" if the question is too personal.) |

Student B

| Ask which course A wants to take. |

| Find out something about A: his/her occupation, major, hobbies, problems. |

| Suggest a specific course that would be appropriate for A's job, major, problems, etc. |

12 🔁
Laugh and learn

Look at the two cartoons. Decide who used a formal way of asking permission, the little boy or Garfield.
Who used an informal way? Which way is more polite?

1. BLONDIE

2. GARFIELD

▶ Would you ask for permission
  with *may* or with *can* in these
  situations?
  Work in pairs. One person asks
  the questions. The other person
  responds.

1 Call your father/boss at work. You know he's in a bad mood, but you really
  need to borrow some money.
2 Call your boyfriend/girlfriend. You want to talk to him/her after class
  tomorrow.
3 Call your father's office. One of his colleagues answers. You want to talk to
  your dad, but he's not in his office at the moment. ›
4 Call home and talk to your brother or sister. You want to speak to your
  mother, but she's not at home.

13 🔁
Role play

Practice these phone conversations. Remember to use *may* in more formal situations.

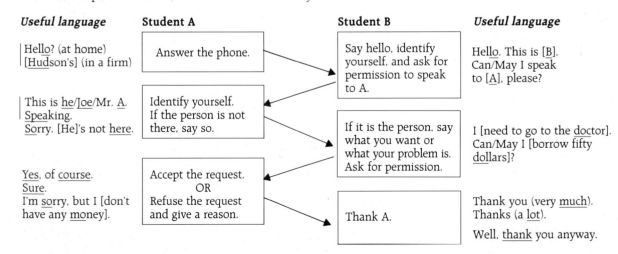

Useful language	Student A	Student B	*Useful language*
Hell<u>o</u>? (at home) [<u>Hudson</u>'s] (in a firm)	Answer the phone.	Say hello, identify yourself, and ask for permission to speak to A.	Hell<u>o</u>. This is [B]. Can/May I speak to [A], please?
This is <u>he</u>/Joe/Mr. <u>A</u>. <u>Speaking</u>. Sorry. [He]'s not <u>here</u>.	Identify yourself. If the person is not there, say so.	If it is the person, say what you want or what your problem is. Ask for permission.	I [need to go to the <u>doctor</u>]. Can/May I [borrow fifty <u>dollars</u>]?
<u>Yes</u>, of <u>course</u>. <u>Sure</u>. I'm <u>sorry</u>, but I [don't have any <u>money</u>].	Accept the request. OR Refuse the request and give a reason.	Thank A.	Thank you (very <u>much</u>). Thanks (a <u>lot</u>). Well, <u>thank</u> you anyway.

14 📼 ⇨
Live from CWHF

A reporter for radio station CWHF is interviewing some people in downtown Montreal. Listen to two of the interviews and complete the chart.

Person interviewed	City of residence	Occupation	Problem at the moment
Kenji Omura			
Heather Spinelli			

▸ Of course, both Kenji and Heather gave the reporter other information too. Rewind the tape, listen again, and take notes. Then work with another student, compare your notes, and ask each other information questions to form a summary of what Kenji and Heather said.

Student B

7 Transfer (page 5)

When Student A asks you a question, choose one of the three choices. Circle it and read it aloud to your partner.

1 a) Before 7.
  b) Between 7 and 8.
  c) After 8.
2 a) Usually.
  b) Sometimes.
  c) Never.
3 a) Rock.
  b) Jazz.
  c) Classical.
4 a) Less than two.
  b) Between two and four.
  c) More than four.
5 a) One, sometimes none.
  b) Two or three.
  c) More than three.
6 a) Less than half an hour.
  b) Between half an hour and an hour and a half.
  c) More than half an hour.
7 a) Before 11.
  b) Between 11 and 12.
  c) After 12.
8 a) No, not at all.
  b) More or less.
  c) Yes, no problem.
9 a) I stayed at home.
  b) I went out.
  c) Sorry, that's personal.
10 a) Yes, and I love to.
  b) Yes, but I hate to.
  c) No, I can't. I don't know how.

▸ Now ask A these questions. Write O.K. when the answer is no problem for you. Find out:

11 How much A smokes.
12 How often A has to borrow money from someone.
13 If A paid the rent on time last month.
14 Who washes the dishes where A lives now.
15 If A sometimes leaves dirty clothes on the floor.
16 How long A usually talks on the phone.
17 How many people called A yesterday.
18 How often A needs to spend an evening alone.
19 If A asks permission before he/she invites people home.
20 If A's friends call before they visit him/her.

▸ After you finish interviewing each other, compare your answers. Count the total number of questions that you wrote O.K. for. Then see what the results mean.

O.K. for at least 13 questions:
Wow! You two are similar in a lot of ways, and you probably would have no problems sharing an apartment.

O.K. for 8 to 12 questions:
Well, you could share the same apartment, but if you can, look for another roommate. You'll be happier.

O.K. for less than 8 questions:
Forget it. You two really are not compatible, so you should not even consider living together. Why look for trouble?

Second unit   Could I try a larger size?

0 ⇄
Warm-up

Work in pairs. Student A thinks of a person in your class. Student B has to guess who it is by asking questions.

A: I'm thinking of a girl/woman/boy/man.
B: What's he/she wearing?
A: He's/She's wearing a [white] [blouse].
              [brown] [slacks].

Other possible questions:

What color is his/her [shirt]?
What color are his/her [shoes]?
Is he/she wearing [white] [socks]?

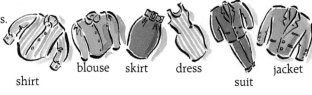

shirt   blouse   skirt   dress   suit   jacket

sweater   hat   slacks jeans   shoes   socks

1 📼
Get ready

Kenji Omura went shopping for some clothes the same afternoon he was interviewed on the radio. When he went into the store, there was only one other customer, a young man from Texas. Listen to Part 1: the conversations between Kenji, the Texan, and the salesclerk. Then answer these four questions:

1 What's the Texan doing?
2 What's Kenji looking for?
3 Which ones are on sale?
4 What kinds of questions might the salesclerk ask Kenji? Make a list of possible questions, and then confirm your guesses when you listen to Part 2 of the dialogue.

2 🔊
Dialogue: Part Two

Listen to Part 2 of the dialogue. Then write **That's right, That's wrong,** or **I don't know** for each sentence.

1 The dark green sweatshirt was under the blue one.
2 Kenji tried on a jacket.
3 Kenji paid more than twenty dollars for the sweatshirt.
4 The clerk lives in the dorm.
5 Kenji and Tex live on the same floor.
6 Tex was not very friendly to Kenji.

3
Focus on new language

Find a word or expression in the dialogue with the same meaning.

Words
1 below
2 the number inside clothing that shows how big it is
3 a piece of glass that reflects images
4 inexpensive

Expressions
5 a way to ask permission (besides "May I," or "Can I")
6 to see if new clothes actually fit
7 being sold at a lower price than usual
8 a more formal way to say "Nice to meet you"

Kenji: Could I see that sweatshirt, please?
Clerk: Which one? This blue one?
K: No, the dark green one right under it.
C: Here you are. It's a 38. What size do you wear?
K: Usually either a 38 or a 40.
C: Would you like to try it on?
K: Yes, I would. It looks a little small.
C: There's a mirror right behind you. You can leave your jacket on this chair here. How does it feel? Is it big enough?
K: I'm not sure. Could I try a larger size?
C: Certainly. Here. This is a 40, a medium. Do you like this one better?
K: Yes, it fits perfectly. How much is it?
C: Well, it was twenty-five dollars, but it's on sale now for just twelve-fifty.
K: That sounds pretty cheap. I'll take it.

K: By the way, do you know where the dining hall is?
C: You mean for dormitory residents? It's kind of hard to explain . . .

Tex: Excuse me, but I'm going there right now. I'd be glad to show you the way.
K: That's very kind of you, but I don't want to delay you.
T: No problem! Let's go. By the way, my name's Jim Bob Travis, but call me Tex, everybody does.
K: How do you do, uh, Tex. I'm Kenji Omura.
T: Nice to meet you, Kenji. Say, do you live in the dorm?
K: Yes, I'm here for the WHF Summer Institute.
T: Well, what do you know! So am I. What part of the dorm are you in?
K: My room's on the third floor.
T: No kidding! That's my floor, too. It looks like we're going to be seeing a lot of each other!
K: Well, that would be very nice.
T: By the way, do you like country and western music? I think . . .

[handwritten notes]
small = pequeño
large = grande
thin = delgado
thick = grueso
soft = suave

4 📼 ⇄

First practice

First, repeat each of these conversations. Then, practice it with other students.

▶ Offer your assistance to someone in a store:
A: May I <u>help</u> you?
B: <u>Yes</u>, please. | I'm looking for | a [winter] [<u>coat</u>].
  | I'd like to see | some [black] [<u>shoes</u>].
  <u>No</u>, thanks. | I'm just <u>looking</u>.

▶ Ask about clothing sizes:
A: What <u>size</u> do you wear?
B: I wear | a [<u>forty</u>].
  I'm | a <u>small</u>/<u>medium</u>/<u>large</u>.

▶ Ask for permission to try something on:
B: May/Could/Can I try | it/them <u>on</u>?
  | a [larger] <u>size</u>?
A: <u>Certainly</u>/<u>Yes</u>, of <u>course</u>.

Could I try it on?
Could I try them on?

▶ Ask about the fit:
A: How | does it | <u>fit</u>?
  | do they | <u>feel</u>?
B: It fits/They fit <u>perfectly</u>/<u>fine</u>
  It feels/seems (a little) <u>small</u>/<u>large</u>.

▶ Ask about price:
B: How much | <u>is</u> it/<u>are</u> they?
  | does it/do they <u>cost</u>?
A: | It's/They're [<u>thirty</u>] [<u>dollars</u>].
  | It <u>was</u>/They <u>were</u> [forty] [dollars], but it's/they're
  on <u>sale</u> now for [<u>thirty</u>].

formal	May I . . . ?
	Could I . . . ?
informal	Can I . . . ?

5

Find the rule

Read this description of the part of the store Kenji is in, and find each object in the picture to the right.

There is a "sale" sign on the wall, and there are some sweatshirts on the table. There is a white sweatshirt under a black one. There is a mirror in the corner between the table and the counter. A chair is beside the counter and a clock is above the "sale" sign. Kenji is in front of the counter, and the salesclerk is behind it. They are in a store.

▶ Where is the ☆ ? Match each symbol with the right preposition.

1 ....e.... above
2 ....h.... behind
3 ....c.... under
4 ....d.... beside
5 ....a.... between
6 ....g.... in
7 ....f.... in front of
8 ....b.... on

a) ▪☆▪   d) ▪☆   f) ▭☆

b) ☆over line   e) ☆   g) 🔲☆

c) ☆over line   ▭   h) ▭☆

Now apply the rule!

Look at the picture of the store again, and write one preposition in each blank.
1 The chair is *between* the counter and the door.
2 There's a poster ...on... the wall.
3 There is a window *beside* the door.
4 There is a box ...under... the window.
5 There are some lights ...above... their heads.
6 There are some tennis rackets ...in... the box.

6 ⇄
Find the differences

Student B: Go to page 17. Your picture shows how this room was yesterday.
Student A: Look at the picture below. It shows how the room looks today. Tell Student B where everything is, and ask B where it was yesterday. Use these words: *above, under, in, on, behind, in front of, between, beside.*
For example: *The books are on the floor, under the chair. Where were they yesterday?*

7 ▱
Focus on pronunciation

Listen to these questions and answers.

A: This sweater looks a little small.

B: Do you like this one better?

A: Yes, it fits perfectly. How much is it?

B: It's only eighty dollars.

▶ Does the voice go up or down at the end of
  a) information questions?
  b) yes/no questions?
  c) statements (normal sentences)?

▶ Does the voice go up or down at the end of these
  sentences? Guess, and then listen to the tape and
  confirm your guesses.

  1 May I help you?
  2 I'm looking for a jacket.
  3 Do you have any white ones?
  4 What size do you wear?
  5 I usually wear a forty.
  6 How does it feel?
  7 Is it big enough?
  8 I think it's perfect.

▶ Now rewind the tape and repeat each sentence.

8 ⇄
Role play

Student B: Go to page 17.
Student A: Imagine that you are in a clothing store.
You'd like to buy some new clothes.

● Say exactly what you are looking for.
● Find out if the store has any on sale now.
● Find out if they have any in the color you want.
● Ask if you can try it/them on.
● It feels/They feel a little small. Ask if you could try a
  larger size.
● Say it feels/they feel fine now.
● Ask about the price.
● Either agree to buy it/them or not. If not, give a
  reason, and thank the clerk.

TAKING STOCK:
A HEALTHY REMINDER

To help you determine the state of your health, the U.S. Department of Health and Human Services developed the self-test below. The test is divided into four sections. Enter your score at the end of each section, and then check to see how you scored.

EATING HABITS

1 I eat a variety of foods each day, such as fruits, vegetables, whole grain breads (not white bread), low fat meats and milk products, and dry peas and beans.

Almost always 4   **Sometimes 1**   **Almost never 0**

2 I limit the amount of fat and cholesterol I eat, including eggs, butter, cream, and fat on meat.

Almost always 2   **Sometimes 1**   **Almost never 0**

3 I limit the amount of salt I eat by cooking with only small amounts and not eating salty snacks.

Almost always 2   **Sometimes 1**   **Almost never 0**

4 I avoid eating too much sugar, especially frequent snacks of candy or soft drinks such as cola.

Almost always 2   **Sometimes 1**   **Almost never 0**

Eating Habits score: _____

EXERCISE AND FITNESS

1 I maintain a desired weight, avoiding both overweight and underweight.

Almost always 3   **Sometimes 1**   **Almost never 0**

2 I do vigorous exercise for 15 to 30 minutes at least three times a week. Examples include running, swimming, and walking fast.

Almost always 3   **Sometimes 1**   **Almost never 0**

3 I do exercises that improve my muscle tone for 15 to 30 minutes three times a week. Examples include yoga, lifting weights, and calisthenics.

Almost always 2   **Sometimes 1**   **Almost never 0**

4 I use part of my free time to participate in family or team activities that increase my level of fitness. Examples include gardening, bowling, and golf.

Almost always 2   **Sometimes 1**   **Almost never 0**

Exercise and Fitness score: _____

STRESS CONTROL

1 I find it easy to relax, and I express my feelings freely.

Almost always 3   **Sometimes 1**   **Almost never 0**

2 I prepare for events or situations that are probably going to be stressful to me.

Almost always 2   **Sometimes 1**   **Almost never 0**

3 I avoid the use of alcohol or other drugs as a way of taking care of stress and problems.

Almost always 3   **Sometimes 1**   **Almost never 0**

4 I have close friends, relatives, others that I can talk to about personal problems and that I can go to for help when I need it.

Almost always 2   **Sometimes 1**   **Almost never 0**

Stress Control score: _____

CIGARETTE SMOKING

1 If you never smoke, automatically give yourself a score of 10 for this section.

2 I smoke only cigarettes that are low in tar and nicotine, or I smoke a pipe or cigars.

Almost always 3   **Sometimes 1**   **Almost never 0**

Smoking score: _____

TOTAL POINTS (all four sections) [   ]

If your score was 35 or more: Excellent! Your answers show that you realize how important health and fitness are.

Scores from 24 to 34: Good! Your health habits in these areas are good, but there is room for improvement too.

Scores from 12 to 23: Your health risks are showing! Maybe you should change some of your habits. Think about it.

Scores of less than 12: You seem to be taking unnecessary risks with your health. The next step is yours.

Read on your own

9 ⇄
Warm-up

What's really healthy? Work in pairs or small groups, and make a list of the five most important ways people can become and stay healthy. Then compare your lists and try to agree on just one list.

- Go jogging every day?
- Get enough sleep?
- Eat a balanced diet?
- Watch your weight?
- Avoid sugar?
- Play tennis?
- Don't smoke?
- Take vitamins?

10
Main ideas

Take the self-test on the previous page and calculate your score. Would the author of the self-test agree with these recommendations? Write **agree** or **disagree** after each one.

1 Eat many different kinds of food every day.
2 Eat as many foods as possible with sugar.
3 Try not to weigh too much or too little.
4 Do hard physical exercise every day.
5 Control stress by smoking and drinking.
6 Discuss your problems with friends and relatives.
7 Avoid thinking about possible problems that you might have in the future.
8 If you really can't quit smoking, smoke a pipe or cigar.

11
Inferences

Look at the self-test again, and see if you can answer these questions.

1 What's the healthiest kind of bread to eat?
2 Why are candy and soft drinks unhealthy?
3 Imagine people whose only exercise is jogging. Why should they do other kinds of exercise too?
4 What's one of the worst ways to reduce stress?
5 According to the self-test, what's the best thing you can do to protect your health?

12
Focus on words

Complete the table with verbs and nouns from the self-test.

Verbs	Nouns
remind	....
weigh	....
....	improvement
....	participation
....	relaxation

13 ⇄
Transfer

Interview your classmates until you find someone who does each of the following things. When someone answers "yes," write his or her name down beside the question.

Find someone who ...
1 Eats at least three vegetables a day.
2 Likes dark bread better than white bread.
3 Drinks lots of water.
4 Never puts salt on his/her food.
5 Is trying to lose weight./Is on a diet.
6 Does some kind of exercise almost every day.
7 Never smokes.
8 Is trying to quit smoking.
9 Enjoys his/her work/classes.
10 Can talk openly to friends or relatives about his/her problems.
11 Is changing his/her life-style (to make it healthier).
12 Got more than 35 points on the self-test.

Do you eat at least three vegetables a day?

No. I don't. Do you?

14
Laugh and learn

In the first cartoon, what is Garfield's owner comparing?
Who does he think is "smarter"?
In the second cartoon, how many things is the little boy
comparing? Does he use the correct comparative form of
quick?

> **Vocabulary notes:**
>
> **is in for something** = is going to get something
> **smart** = intelligent
> **quick** = fast
> **brain** = the large organ inside the head that permits us
> to think.

1. GARFIELD

2. PEANUTS

Can you remember the rules for forming comparative
forms of adjectives? Look at these examples and try to
state the rules. Be sure to count the number of syllables
first.

1 cheap → cheap**er**
2 important → **more** important
3 healthy → health**ier**

15 ⇨
Tic-tac-toe

Student A is X, and Student B is O.
Try to make a true statement about health or fitness, using
the comparative form of the adjectives in the boxes. For
example, if Student A says *Running is faster than walking*,
he puts an X on the word *fast*. The goal is to mark three
X's or three O's in a row, across, down or from one corner
to the other.

fast	dangerous	salty
good	easy	safe
healthy	bad	interesting

► Work in pairs. Compare the things below.
  Student A: Make a comparison.
  Student B: Ask why A thinks so.
  Student A: Give a reason for your opinion.

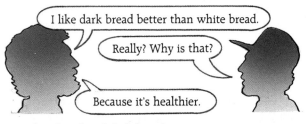

1 white bread and dark bread
2 fruit and cake
3 swimming and lifting weights
4 losing weight and gaining weight
5 juice and soft drinks
6 starting to smoke and quitting smoking

16 🎞️
Live from CWHF

Tex's favorite country and western singer, Loretta Sue Cline, is giving an interview on the radio. Listen and find out the following information.

1 The reason Loretta Sue is in Montreal.
2 How long she's planning to stay.
3 The name of her newest hit record.
4 What her songs are usually about.
5 Where and when she was born.
6 Where she grew up.
7 How she got started singing.
8 Her plans for the future.

▶ What is Loretta Sue singing about? Listen again; then fill in the blanks to complete the words of the song.

I was sitting home the other night

Watching the .... show.

The kids were .... in their beds,

And .... was feeling real low.

At half past three you still .... home

I said I just don't ....

But I can't, no I can't, can't take it anymore

Cuz I'm .... , getting ....

Of living on my own.

.... of working and worrying,

.... of being so ....

Student B

6 Find the differences *(page 13)*

Your picture shows how this room was yesterday, and Student A's picture shows how the room looks today. Tell Student A where everything was yesterday, and ask A where it is now.

Use these words: *above, under, in, on, behind, in front of, between, beside.*

For example: *The books were on the desk yesterday. Where are they now?*

8 Role play *(page 13)*

Imagine that you are a salesclerk in a clothing store, and Student A comes into the store to buy some new clothes. Before you begin, look at the things that are on sale (in the box).

• Offer Mr./Ms. A your assistance.
• Tell A what kinds of things you have on sale.
• Find out what color and size A wants.
• Find out if A wants to try it/them on.
• Ask A how it/they feel.
• When A asks about the price, tell him/her, but try to convince him/her to buy the clothes.
• If A buys something, try to sell him/her something else.
• If A doesn't buy anything, invite him/her to come back again soon. Say goodbye politely.

ALL SIZES
white, blue, yellow
$14.99 each
(were $29.99)

ALL SIZES
gray, black, brown
$29/pair
(were $49/pair)

SMALL SIZES ONLY
green, white, gray
$24.95 each
(were $34.95)

ALL SIZES EXCEPT SMALL
all colors except blue
and white
$35 each (were $60)

Third unit
The strangest thing happened . . .

0
Warm-up

What's happening in these pictures? What are the people doing?

1 🔲
Get ready

Jean and Heather are telling Marta about a strange experience they had that afternoon. Listen to Part 1 of their conversation. Then answer these five questions.

1 Why is Jean a "nervous wreck"?
2 Where did the accident happen?
3 Who caused it?
4 What did he give Jean?
5 Why?

Heather: Are you going out, Marta?

Marta: Yes, I'm going to meet Diane. We're going bicycle riding. Want to come?

H: Thanks, but I'd better stay here. Hey, what's that on your leg?

M: Oh, that. It's just a scar – a reminder of the most unlucky day of my life.

H: Really? What happened?

M: Well, it was two years ago, one day during final exam week at the university. I had my hardest test early in the morning, and afterwards I was really tense, so I decided to go jogging to relax. But when I was running along the street, a dog started chasing me.

H: What kind of dog was it? Was it big?

M: Not too big, but the littlest dogs sometimes have the sharpest teeth!

H: Did it catch you? Is that how you hurt your leg?

M: No, I ran into a building, and the dog went away after a while.

H: Oh, Marta. It probably thought you were just playing. So you got home O.K., right?

M: *Almost.* When I was going up in the elevator, there was a power failure. I couldn't believe it!

H: Neither can I! Don't tell me you got stuck between floors.

M: Yes. And the most frightening thing was that I was all alone, and in the dark. So I began shouting for help, and finally somebody heard me. It was awful.

H: Did you have to stay in there long?

M: Only the longest fifteen minutes of my life.

H: Wait a minute, Marta. You still didn't tell me how you got that scar.

M: That's the craziest part of the whole story. It was dark inside my apartment, and I couldn't see a thing. So, of course I tripped, broke a flower vase, fell and cut my leg on the broken glass.

H: That's a *lot* of bad luck, Marta. Did all that *really* happen?

M: Well . . .

H: Anyway, how did you do on the test?

M: Ha, ha. I'll bet you think I failed, but I didn't! I got the highest score! That's not luck, though. That's *brains.*

2 🔲
Dialogue: Part Two

There is an information error in each sentence. Correct it after you listen to Part 2 of the dialogue.

1 Heather accepts Marta's invitation.
2 Marta was jogging when a dog started biting her.
3 Marta ran into a building to rest.
4 Marta was in the elevator with eleven people in the dark.
5 Marta cut her leg on a piece of metal.
6 Marta failed her test.

3
Focus on new language

Find a word or expression in the dialogue with the same meaning.

Words
1 a mark on the skin caused by an accident or by surgery
2 at a later time
3 past of "can't"
4 as a result, consequently
5 intelligence

Expressions
6 leaving the house
7 I should
8 left, disappeared
9 a blackout (no electricity)
10 you probably think

4
First practice

With another student talk about what
happened in each picture. Have
conversations like the one in the
example to the right. Use your
imagination; there are many possible
explanations for each picture.

A: What happened to <u>him</u>?
B: He [fell <u>down</u>].
A: How did it <u>happen</u>?
B: He was [<u>running</u>] when
   [somebody <u>pushed</u> him].
A: What did he do after <u>that</u>?
B: He [stood <u>up</u> and started
   running again].

5
Find the rule

Look at these sentences:

Event	Surrounding action
We had an accident There was a power failure	when we were driving home. when I was going up in the elevator.

▶ Which part of the sentence is the most important?   a) The event.
                                                      b) The surrounding action.

▶ Which part tells what was going on at the same time?   a) The event.
                                                         b) The surrounding action.

▶ Which verb tense do we use to describe the surrounding action?   a) Simple past.
                                                                   b) Past continuous.

▶ What is the formula for information questions in the past continuous tense?
   For example: *What were you doing*?   a) WV?
                                         b) WASV?

Now apply the rules!

First, classify each of these sentences as either E (an event) or SA (a surrounding action).

1 .... He met Jean

2 .... It started to rain.

3 .... I was watching TV.

4 .... Jean heard someone call her name.

5 .... We were playing tennis.

6 .... She was waiting for Heather.

7 .... You called.

8 .... Yves was jogging.

▶ Now make four sentences by combining one event and one surrounding action with *when*, For example:
   Yves was jogging when he met Jean. or *When Yves was jogging, he met Jean.*

6
How good is your memory?

Jean, Marta, and Diane gave a party the other night. Someone took this picture at 1 A.M.

Student B: Study the picture for thirty seconds. Then go to page 25.

Student A: While Student B is looking at page 25, ask him/her about these actions/people.

- playing guitar
- singing
- opening door
- going in
- smoking
- eating
- holding a glass
- sleeping
- Yves
- Jean
- Heather
- Kenji
- Marta
- Diane
- Tex

For example: *Who was sleeping? Where was Kenji? What was he doing?*

7 📼
Focus on pronunciation

We can say the same sentence in different ways depending on what we want to emphasize. Notice which words are stressed (emphasized) in this conversation.

Yves: Hello, Jean. How <u>are</u> you?
Jean: I'm <u>fine</u>. How are <u>you</u>?
Yves: I'm fine <u>too</u>, thanks.

▶ Listen to this conversation, and underline the syllable with the most stress in each sentence or phrase.

1 What's your name?
2 Jack Davis. What's your name?
3 Sally Jankowski. It's nice to meet you, Jack.
4 It's nice to meet you, Sally.
5 What do you do?
6 I'm an architect. What do you do?
7 I work in a big bank.
8 I work in the National Bank, in fact.

▶ Now rewind the tape, and repeat each sentence.

8
Role play

Student A: You are a teenager, and you told your parents that you were going to study at a friend's house. Actually, the friend was giving a big party that night, and you got home very late. You didn't have any books, and you were wearing "party" clothes. But don't panic. Think of a good story to tell your parents.

Student B: Your son/daughter told you that he/she was going to a friend's house to study and promised to be home before 10 P.M. You waited impatiently until past midnight when he/she finally walked in. You are furious. Of course, you want to know what he/she was doing all evening. Have a "serious" talk with your son/daughter, but control yourself!

From *The Guinness Book of Records*

The Human Being

- People come in all shapes and sizes, of course. Take Robert Wadlow, for example. When he was born, he weighed 8½ pounds (3.86 kg.) but by the time he ws 21, his weight was up to 491 pounts (223 kg.). He was 8 feet 11 inches (2.72 m.) tall: the tallest person who has ever lived. He was strong too: at age 9 he carried his father up the stairs of their home in Alton (USA).

Diana Ross   Tom Selleck

Robert Wadlow

Shigechiyo Izumi

- Some entertainers earn huge amounts of money for performing. The highest-paid performer is Dolly Parton, an American country and western singer. She gets $400,000 for a live concert. The best-paid television actor is Tom Selleck, who earns $220,000 for each episode of the detective series "Magnum, P.I." Financially speaking, the most successful movie star today is Sylvester Stallone, who has already received over $20 million for *Rambo*.

Human Achievements

- People set records for many reasons. For example, the longest engagement on record was 67 years. Octavio Guillen and Adriana Martinez finally got married in Mexico City when they were both 82.
- In sports, records are constantly being broken, but here are some not-so-recent achievements. Patrick J. McDonald was the oldest athlete ever to win an Olympic gold medal. He was 42, and that was in 1920. The youngest winner of the Wimbledon Singles in tennis was only 15 years old at the time – in 1887. Her name was Charlotte Dod. And the athlete who won the largest number of gold medals in the Olympics was Ray Ewry, who won 10 times between 1900 and 1908 for long jump, high jump, standing jump and triple jump.

Charlotte Dod

- Lots of people have claimed to be extremely old, but they usuallly can't prove their claims. The greatest authenticated age that anyone has ever lived to is 120 years, 237 days in the case of Shigechiyo Izumi of Asan, Japan. He was born in 1865, and in 1871 Japan's first census recorded him as a 6-year-old. He died in 1986.

The Arts and Entertainment

- Artists and entertainers are part of a world of superlatives. Currently, the word's best-selling author is Barbara Cartland, with global sales of 400,000,000 copies for 418 different books, published in 17 languages. In 1986 alone, she published 26 new novels.
- In the world of popular music, records often last only a short time. Although it is difficult to estimate the size of crowds at open-air concerts, Diana Ross claims the record for the biggest audience. Over 800,000 people supposedly attended her concert in New York's Central Park in 1983.

Read on your own

9 ⇄
Warm-up

Think about people you know or know about. Then play tic-tac-toe with another student using the words in the boxes. Ask each other questions like *Who is the tallest person in your family?* and *Where does the richest person in the world live?* You get an X or an O if you ask the question correctly.

tallest	most athletic	richest
most generous	funniest	most creative
strongest	most successful	kindest

10
Specific information

Look at the page to the left, and find the answers to these questions. Work as fast as you can.

1 Who has written more than 400 books?
2 What is the largest audience that has ever attended an outdoor concert?
3 How old was Shigechiyo Izumi when he died?
4 How much does Dolly Parton receive for every live concert?
5 When did Ray Ewry win his Olympic gold medals?
6 How tall was Robert Wadlow?
7 Why were Octavio Guillen and Adriana Martinez record-breakers?

11
Vocabulary in context

Match the words in italics in these sentences with the definitions.

a) an agreement to get married later
b) at the present time
c) very large
d) large concentrations of people
e) more than
f) surpassed, exceeded
g) until now, so far
h) went to, were present at

1 .... He was the tallest person who *ever* lived.

2 .... *Currently*, the world's best-selling author is Barbara Cartland.

3 .... It is difficult to estimate the size of *crowds* at open-air concerts.

4 .... Over 800,000 people supposedly *attended* her concert.

5 .... Some entertainers earn *huge* amounts of money . . .

6 .... Sylvester Stallone has already received *over* $20 million . . .

7 .... The longest *engagement* on record is 67 years.

8 .... In sports, records are constantly being *broken* . . .

12 ⇄
Role play

Student A: Imagine that you are the oldest person in your country (over one hundred). Make a list of some of the most important things that happened during your lifetime. For example, write down famous inventions, wars, celebrations, disasters, and happy events, e.g. *There were two world wars. Humans went to the moon.*

Student B: Imagine that you are a reporter, and you are going to interview the oldest person in your country, Mr./Ms. A. Ask this old man/woman about his/her memories of famous events that happened during his/her lifetime. Before you begin, make a list of the questions you'd like to ask Mr./Ms. A.

13

Laugh and learn

1. PEANUTS

In the first cartoon, why does the letter Snoopy receives say "This is the *dumbest* story" rather than "the *dumber* story"? What is the smallest number of stories the editor has read?

In the second cartoon, Peppermint Patty makes a grammatical mistake. What should she say instead of "best"?

2. PEANUTS

The rules for forming the comparative and superlative forms of adjectives are identical except for the markers each uses: comparative = *more* + adjective or adjective + *er*; superlative = *the most* + adjective or the adjective + *est*.

▶ Look at the examples and decide what the missing forms are.

1 tall – taller – the tallest
2 big – bigger – the ...biggest...
3 rich – ...richer... – ...the richest...
4 easy – easier – the easiest
5 happy – happier – the ...happiest...
6 rainy – ...rainier... – ...the rainiest...
7 boring – more boring – the most boring

8 successful – more successful – the ...most successful...
9 interesting – ...more interesting... – the most interesting

▶ What are the rules?
a) For adjectives with one syllable, add ...er... or ...est... .

b) For adjectives with two syllables ending in **y**, add ...ier... or ...iest... . For other adjectives, use ...more... or ...the most... .

14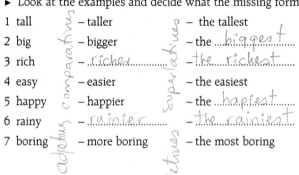

Share information

The table below compares several international cities. Work with another student. First ask and answer questions to complete the table. Then discuss which city is the largest/closest to New York, and which has the cheapest movies.
Student A: Complete the table on this page.
Student B: Your table is on page 25.

Student B: Your table is on page 25.

> **Useful language**
> How <u>big</u> is [Montreal]?
> How much does a <u>movie</u> cost?
> How long does it take to get to New <u>York</u>?

City	Population	Flight time to N.Y.	Cost of a movie (US$)
Montreal		1 hour 30 minutes	
Los Angeles	7,818,000		$6.00
Mexico City		4 hours 15 minutes	
São Paulo	13,000,000		$3.00
London			$7.00
Madrid	3,188,297		
Tokyo		12 hours 20 minutes	$10.00

How much does a tire cost?

15 📼
Live from CWHF

Last night people reported seeing UFO's (unidentified flying objects). You are going to hear Marie Dubonnet's interview with one of those people. Listen for the answers to these questions.

1 What was Mr. Benson doing when the UFO landed?
2 What happened to his car while he was driving it into the garage?
3 What other things convinced him that something was happening?
4 What did he see coming out of the UFO?
5 What did Mr. Benson say about the red ball?
6 What was happening to the dog?

▶ Listen again to the interview, paying special attention to Mr. Benson's description of the UFO. Then make a quick drawing of it, and compare drawings with your classmates.

Student B

6 How good is your memory?
(page 21)

Here is the outline of the picture you saw on page 21. Look at it while Student A is asking you questions about what was happening when the picture was taken.

14 Share information *(page 24)*

The table below compares several international cities. Work with another student. First ask and answer questions to complete the table. Then discuss which city is the largest/closest to New York, and which has the cheapest movies.

> **Useful language**
> How <u>big</u> is [Montreal]?
> How much does a <u>mo</u>vie cost?
> How long does it take to get to New <u>York</u>?

City	Population	Flight time to N.Y.	Cost of a movie (US$)
Montreal	2,862,300		$5.00
Los Angeles		6 hours 54 minutes	
Mexico City	17,000,000		$1.00
São Paulo		10 hours 35 minutes	
London	9,012,700	6 hours	
Madrid		7 hours 30 minutes	$4.00
Tokyo	15,687,141		

Fourth unit What are you going to do?

0 ⇄
Warm-up

Talk to as many people as possible and find out who has the most interesting plans for tonight. Make a list using their answers. Find out:

- What they're doing tonight.
- Where they're doing it.
- Who they're doing it with.
- What time and how long they plan to do it.
- How often they do this.

Interview your teacher first.

NAME	ACTIVITY	PLACE	WITH	TIME

1 ▭
Get ready

It's Thursday evening, and Jean and Heather are at home when the phone rings. Listen to Part 1 of their conversation. Then answer these five questions.

1 What does Yves want to know? *If Jean is free*
2 What does he want to do? *to talk to Jean*
3 What does Jean promise?
4 What is Heather going to do now? *going to bed*
5 What does Heather offer to do for Jean? *Translate*

Jean: O.K., Yves, what's this all about?

Yves: Tell me, Jean. What are you going to do this weekend? Got any plans?

J: Gee, I really don't know yet. I was planning to do some studying. And I really should take Heather shopping for some new shoes. Why?

Y: Well, Tex, Kenji, and I are thinking about going to Mont Tremblant on Saturday.

J: Oh, yeah? What are you guys going to do up there?

Y: We'd like to go rafting on the Rouge River. The problem is that we need six people in order to rent the raft. And we thought you, Diane, and Marta might like to go with us.

J: Me? In a rubber raft miles from nowhere? Are you out of your mind?

Y: Oh, come on. It's not dangerous. You're not afraid of a little cold water, are you?

J: No, I guess not. Not if it's in a glass.

Y: And you can swim pretty well, can't you?

J: Well, I could the last time I tried, but gee, that was a few years ago, and . . .

Y: Good! So you're going with us, right?

J: Wait. Not so fast. We still need to find out if Diane and Marta want to go, don't we?

Y: No, don't worry. I talked to them already.

J: Hmph. I smell a conspiracy. Anyway, who would stay with Heather? And
. . .

Heather: Oh, Mom! I forgot to ask. Can I stay overnight with my friend Michelle? Her mom says it's all right. We're going to practice the "rap." It's a dance.

J: Heather! I thought you were watching television. I don't know what I'm going to do with you.

H: I don't either. That's why I thought I'd better keep one ear open.

J: Sometimes it's not easy being a single parent, believe me.

H: Is it harder than being an only child?

2 🔲
Dialogue: Part Two

Listen to Part 2 of the dialogue. Then write **That's right**, **That's wrong**, or **I don't know** for each sentence.

1 Heather needs some new shoes.
2 Yves goes rafting almost every weekend.
3 Yves owns his own raft.
4 Jean knows how to swim.
5 Diane and Marta know about the raft trip.
6 Michelle is the same age as Heather.

3
Focus on new language

Find a word or expression in the dialogue with the same meaning.

Words
1 men, boys (*informal*)
2 past of *can* (indicating ability)
3 also or too – after a negative expression
4 father or mother

Expressions
5 are you crazy?
6 a small number of
7 sleep at someone else's house
8 a person without any brothers or sisters.

4 🔲 ⇄

First practice

First, repeat each of these conversations. Then, practice it with other students.

▶ Ask and answer questions about your future plans or intentions:

A: What are you going to do
  | this/next <u>week</u>end/<u>sum</u>mer?
  | to<u>mor</u>row?

B: | I'm going to | take a <u>trip</u>/va<u>ca</u>tion.
  | | go out of <u>town</u>.
  | | go to the <u>mov</u>ies/a <u>con</u>cert/a <u>play</u>.
  | I don't <u>know</u> yet.

▶ If the person has plans, find out where he or she plans to go:

A: Where are you going to <u>go</u>? / Where are you <u>go</u>ing?

B: I'm going (to go) to [Que<u>bec</u>] / [the Roxy <u>The</u>ater] / [Joe's <u>Jazz</u> Club].

▶ Find out who he or she plans to go with:

A: Are you going (to go) <u>alone</u>/<u>with</u> someone?

B: | I'm going with [Jean].
  | Yes, I <u>am</u>.
  | I'm not <u>sure</u> yet.

▶ Find out how he or she is planning to get there:

A: How are you going to <u>get</u> there?

B: | By <u>car</u>/<u>bus</u>/<u>train</u>/<u>plane</u>/<u>sub</u>way.
  | I'm going to <u>drive</u>/<u>fly</u>/take a [<u>bus</u>]/<u>walk</u>.

▶ Continue the conversation by asking and answering other questions. For example:

Do you always go to . . . [on weekends]?
Why did you decide to go to . . . ?
How far is . . . from here?
Did you go there last [weekend] too?
Where did you go last . . . ?
Do you like . . . better than . . . ?
When are you going to come back?

5

Find the rule

You already know how to talk about future plans and intentions by using the present continuous.
For example: *Where are you going next weekend?*
       We're driving to Mont Tremblant on Saturday.

▶ What part of the sentence tells us that the action is in the future?
  a) the verb tense
  b) the time expression

We talk about future plans and intentions in another way, too. Look at these sentences.

W	A	S	*going to*	V	(O)
What	are	you	going to	do	next weekend?
	Are	you	going to	see	your family?
	Is	Jean	going to	try	it too?

S	A	*going to*	V	(O)
I	am	going to	take	a trip.
I	am	going to	go	rafting.
She	is	going to	think	about it.

▶ What form of the verb comes after *going to*?
  a) a conjugated verb (I walk, she walks, etc.)
  (b) a simple verb (no endings)

▶ What is the auxiliary verb?
  a) *be*
  (b) *going*

▶ Which of these sentences *clearly* talks about future plans or intentions?
  a) We're giving a party.
  (b) We're going to give a party.

Now apply the rule!

This is part of a letter than Jean wrote to a friend. Write the correct forms of *be* + verb + *ing* or *be* + *going to* + verb.

Guess what? I (do) 'm going to do something really exciting on Saturday. Five of my friends and I (drive) _____ up to Mont Tremblant, a beautiful park, north of Montreal. We (rent) _____ a rubber raft and then go down the river in it. I can't wait! Heather (stay) _____ with one of her friends that day. Tell me, when (you/come) _____ up here to see us? I hope it's soon. That's all for now. I (drop) _____ this at the post office on the way to the gym.

6
Transfer

Work in groups of three. First, fill in the appointment book with your plans for next weekend. Be sure to write the approximate time of each activity too. For example, you might be planning to study, go shopping, play tennis, visit friends, go out with someone, sleep late, watch something special on TV, go to church, or have lunch with your family.

Then, ask one another questions about your plans, and find a time when all three of you would be free for at least one hour. Finally, decide what the three of you are going to do then!

APPOINTMENTS	SATURDAY	SUNDAY
A.M		
Noon		
Afternoon		
Evening		

Functions

- Find out his/her plans for a specific day and time.
- If necessary, find out if he/she has plans for another day and time.
- If necessary, say you're not free and give the reason.
- Suggest getting together at a specific time.

Useful language

What are you going to do on [Saturday morning]?
Are you going to be busy between [12 and 2] on [Saturday]?
I'm sorry, but I can't then. I'm going to [study].
Let's get together on [Sunday] at [six o'clock].

7 📼
Focus on pronunciation

Americans pronounce *going to* as /gonna/ in certain kinds of sentences. Listen to these two sentences:

1 I'm going to the movies tonight.
2 I'm going to go to the movies tonight.

▸ In which sentence did he pronounce *going to* as /gonna/? In sentence 1 or sentence 2?

▸ In sentence 1, there is a place (*the movies*) right after *going to*, but in sentence 2, there is an action (*go*) after *going to*. When do Americans say /gonna/?

▸ Look at these sentences. Guess in which sentences *going to* is pronounced, as /gonna/. Then listen to the tape and confirm your guesses.

1 Where are you going?
2 I'm going to go to the park.
3 What are you going to do there?
4 I'm going to run.
5 Well, I'm going to go swimming.
6 But it's going to rain soon.
7 I'm going to an indoor pool.

▸ Rewind the tape and repeat each sentence.

8 ⇄
Role play

Student B: Go to page 33.
Student A: You're going on vacation, taking the tour described on the right. You'd really like to spend your vacation with Student B. Find out B's plans. Try to convince B to go with you – or change your mind and go with B!

Find out:
- Where B is going to go.
- Where B is going to stay.
- How long B is going to stay there.
- How much B is going to pay.
- What B is going to do during the day . . . and at night.
- Ask B why he/she doesn't come with you instead. Tell B that he/she really should!
- Give reasons why Taormina is better and why B should spend his/her vacation there.

Tour 29: Taormina, Sicily

Hotel Etna Palace (★★★★) – *on the beach. 2 weeks for just $985 – air fare included!*

Beautiful, modern rooms, each with:
- Color TV (6 channels: 4 Italian 2 English)
- 24-hour room service
- Air-conditioning

☐ *take an Italian course* ☐ *visit Roman ruins*
☐ *learn to water-ski* ☐ *meet people from all*
☐ *lie on the beach all day* *over Europe and*
☐ *dance all night long* *North Africa*
☐ *eat Sicilian food*

Working moms

1 Today, more women than ever before are combining the traditional role of mother with that of **breadwinner**. Nearly two-thirds of all the mothers in the United States have a job outside the home. About half of all mothers have full-time jobs and more than half of women who have babies go back to their jobs before their child is one year old.

2 Many of these working mothers are happy being part of the work force and bringing up their children and feel **proud** that they combine the two roles successfully. However, some also feel **guilty** because they do not have more time to spend with their kids. They also complain of stress and **lack** of leisure time. We asked working mothers to write to us and tell us what their lives are like. More than a thousand women replied. Here are some of their stories:

3 Julie Lomasky went back to her job as an administration executive at a large New England hospital less than a week after her baby was born. "I think that I'm a better mother because I work," she says. She feels that some of her **worth** comes from her job, just as some of it comes from being a wife and mother. Rebecca Hoffman, a grade school teacher and mother of two small boys in Ohio says she wouldn't quit her job even if she was offered a million dollars! As she says, "I love my job. I would go **nuts** if I had to stay at home all day." For both Julie and Rebecca, not working is out of the question.

4 Linda Sullivan from Seattle, Washington has two children, Greg, 11 and Meredith, 9. When Linda and her husband, Gary, got divorced the children were ages 3 and 1. Linda went back to school and got a **degree** in engineering. She has been working full time for five years now and she supports herself and the children on what she earns as an engineer at a large manufacturing company. Most single mothers like Linda work because they have to.

5 In contrast, Dorothy Johnson is happily married, has a full-time job and takes care of her two children, Kelsie, 9, and Kendra, 5. She gets up at 6:30 A.M. every day, cooks a hot breakfast for her husband and kids and braids her daughters' hair. At 7:30 she drives the kids to school and then hurries to her job as assistant principal at Columbus Junior High School.

6 Dorothy and her family live in a pleasant suburb southwest of Baltimore. When she and Rich got married they had very little money. "Now", she says, "we like to live in a nice area, buy good things and take the kids on vacation. My salary helps us to do all this." The Johnsons need two incomes in order to maintain the pleasant life-style they want to have.

7 Dorothy also values the financial independence that she gets from her job. She says it helps her to feel good about herself and she hopes that her children **look up to** her as someone who can take care of herself. She says "If anything ever happens to Rich, I know that I can still **survive**."

Read on your own

9 ⇄
Warm-up

Are you, your mother, or your wife a working mother?

Divide up into groups and discuss the daily routines of working mothers you know well. As you talk, make a list of all the activities they do, or what they did on a specific day, like last Tuesday.

gets up – 6.30
washes face and hands
makes coffee
gets the newspaper
walks the dog

10
Main ideas

Read the article "Working moms" and classify these statements as T (true) or F (false).

1 Most mothers in the U.S. work.
2 Most women wait until their children are five before going back to work.
3 Many mothers work in order to avoid their children.
4 Julie Lomasky and Rebecca Hoffman hate their jobs.
5 Linda Sullivan is a single parent.
6 Dorothy Johnson takes good care of her children.
7 Mr. and Mrs. Johnson both work so that they can have a good life-style.
8 Mrs. Johnson has a positive self-image.

11
Topic sentences

Most paragraphs have a topic sentence: one sentence that gives the main idea of that entire paragraph. Find the topic sentence in these paragraphs of "Working moms."

1 Paragraph 3   a) Sentence 1 ("Julie Lomasky went . . .")
                b) Sentence 2 ("I think that I'm . . .")
                c) Last sentence ("For both Julie . . .")

2 Paragraph 4   a) Sentence 1 ("Linda Sullivan . . .")
                b) Sentence 3 ("Linda went back . . .")
                c) Last sentence ("Most single mothers . . .")

3 Paragraph 5   a) Sentence 1 ("In contrast, Dorothy . . .")
                b) Sentence 2 ("She gets up . . .")
                c) Last sentence ("At 7:30 she . . .")

12
Vocabulary in context

There are nine words highlighted in the article. Read the sentences they are part of again and match each one with the right definition.

1 breadwinner (paragraph 1)   a) absence
2 proud (paragraph 2)   b) responsible for something negative
3 guilty (paragraph 2)   c) crazy (*slang*)
4 lack (paragraph 2)   d) continue living
5 worth (paragraph 3)   e) pleased with some action
6 nuts (paragraph 3)   f) person who supports family financially
7 degree (paragraph 4)   g) respect, admire
8 look up to (paragraph 7)   h) a university diploma
9 survive (paragraph 7)   i) value

13 ⇄
Role play

Student A: Imagine that you are a married woman with one small child. You have a college degree and worked before you got married. Now you want to go back to work, but your husband doesn't like the idea. Convince him that you are right. Finally, decide what you are going to do.

Student B: Imagine you are Student A's husband. You have one child, and you would like one more. Your wife wants to start working again, but you think she should stay at home with your child. Convince her that you are right. But don't get angry if she doesn't agree with you!

14
Laugh and learn

Adverbs of manner usually answer the question *How?* or *In what way?*

▶ In the first cartoon, can you find two adverbs? What does each one refer to?
   (In what way should Garfield diet? How should he look at food?)
▶ In the second cartoon, there is an adverb too, but it does not end in **-ly**. What is it?
   What does it refer to? (How does Garfield eat?)
▶ What do adverbs of manner describe?   a) things   b) actions

1. GARFIELD

2. GARFIELD

15 ⇄
Using adverbs

Work in pairs. Student A reads the sentence. Student B makes an appropriate comment that has a verb and an adverb. Use the adverbs in the box. Finally, Student A makes an appropriate comment related to what Student B said. Look at these two examples:

Example: Joe had a car accident yesterday.
          A: Joe had a car accident yesterday.
          B: That's too bad, but I'm not surprised. He drives really badly.
          A: He sure does. He's the worst driver I know.

Example: Marta won a prize at the disco the other night.
          A: Marta won a prize at the disco the other night.
          B: That's great, but I'm not surprised. She dances really well.
          A: I think so too. She's a wonderful dancer.

1 Yves volunteered as an English-French interpreter at the Summer Institute.
2 Heather is still reading the same book that she started a month ago.
3 Jean's Italian is so good that everyone thinks she's Italian.
4 Kenji ran ten kilometers in just half an hour yesterday.
5 Jean's ex-husband never stops working.
6 Yves and Kenji are afraid to ride with Tex in his car.
7 Heather almost never has any mistakes in her homework.
8 Everybody is buying Loretta Sue's new record.
9 Kenji had to fire his secretary because of her typing.
10 Diane and Marta got to the concert too late to get tickets.

Adverbs
badly
beautifully
carefully
dangerously
fast
fluently
hard
late
perfectly
slowly
well

16 📼
Live from CWHF

Let's listen to the news on radio station CWHF. Before you listen, look at each picture and read the questions under it. Try to guess what each of these four news stories is about.

1 What kind of operation did the man have?
2 What surprise is he going to have soon?

3 What does Benjamin Franklin have to do with this story?
4 When did someone borrow the book?

5 What is the new rule at Veterans High School?
6 Why did school officials make the rule?

7 Why was the man angry?
8 What did he try to change?

▶ Listen to the four news stories again, and then try to retell them in your own words.

Student B

8 Role play (page 29)

You're going on vacation, taking the tour described here. You'd really like to spend your vacation with Student A. Find out A's plans. Try to convince A to go with you – or change your mind and go with A!

Find out:
- Where A is going to go on vacation.
- Where A is going to stay.
- How long A is going to stay there.
- How much A is going to pay.
- What A is going to do during the day . . . and at night.
- Ask A why he/she doesn't come with you instead. Tell A that he/she really should!
- Give reasons why Tahiti is better and why A should spend his/her vacation there.

Tour 12: Tahiti

Hotel Southern Cross (★★★) – on the beach. 10 days for just $1,240 – air fare included!

Comfortable, modern rooms, each with:
- Color TV: 2 channels (both in French)
- Mini-refrigerator
- View of the ocean

☐ take a French course
☐ learn to scuba dive
☐ lie on the beach all day
☐ meet people from all over the world
☐ learn to hula dance
☐ visit Polynesian villages
☐ dance until midnight

Grammar review game:
Around the world

Warm-up:

Work with a partner to match these cities with the descriptions.

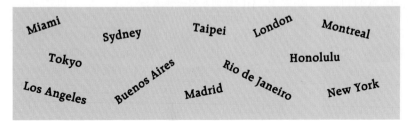

- This is the oldest and largest city in Australia. It is famous for its modern opera house.

- This is the second largest French-speaking city in the world, and it's in Canada! Visit the historic "old" city on an island in the St. Lawrence River.

- In this city you can go to the Kabukiza, the traditional Japanese theater. The snow-covered Mount Fuji is about 100 miles away.

- The capital city of England is famous for its rainy weather. Two popular tourist attractions are Westminster Abbey and Buckingham Palace.

- You can watch a bullfight, the national Spanish spectacle, in this city. When you are there, visit the Prado Museum.

- This American city on the Atlantic Ocean is well known for its warm sunny weather and its beautiful beaches. Spanish is one of the official languages of the city.

- This South American capital on the Rio de la Plata river looks like a European city. Go to one of the city's tango clubs to see professional dancers perform.

- The heart of this American city is the island of Manhattan. The headquarters of the United Nations are here. And, of course, so is the Statue of Liberty.

- This city is the capital of Taiwan, Republic of China. The National Museum there has thousands of pieces of Chinese art.

- The capital city of the state of Hawaii is on Oahu Island in the Pacific Ocean. The Hawaii Volcanoes National Park has some of the largest and most active volcanoes in the world.

- This city in South America is famous for Carnival and dancing samba in the streets. Soccer is also important. You can see a game at Maracanã, the world's largest stadium.

- This city is the home of Hollywood, the world capital of the movie and television industry. The best way to see the city is by car; it covers over 450 square miles!

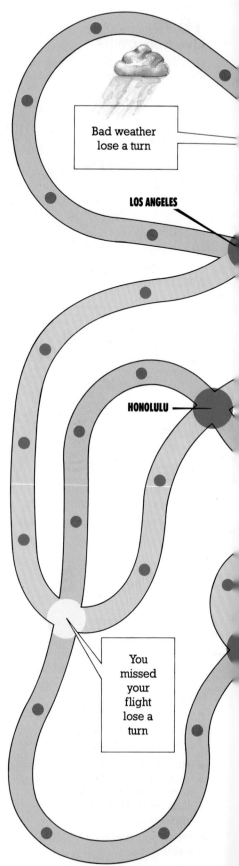

Bad weather lose a turn

LOS ANGELES

HONOLULU

You missed your flight lose a turn

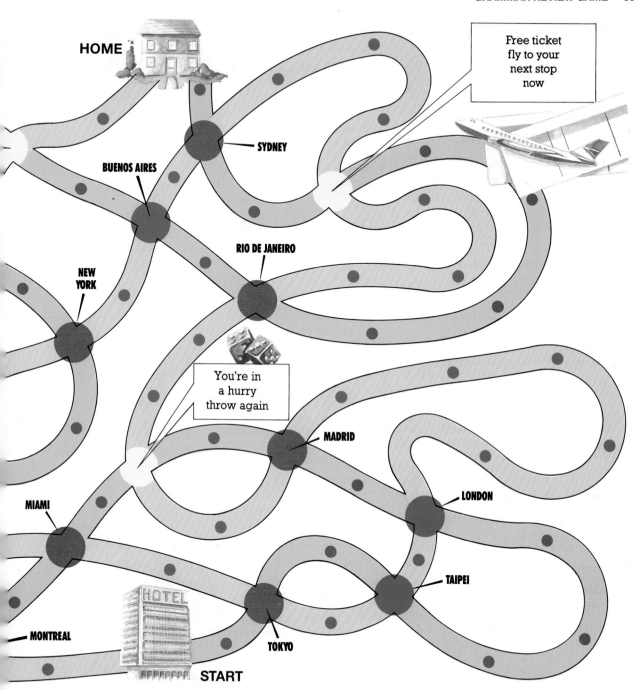

Rules:

1. Work in pairs. Use coins as markers.

2. Toss a coin. If heads, go forward TWO spaces; if tails, go ONE space.

3. Student A must stop at all RED cities; Student B must go to all BLUE cities. You do not need to go to your partner's cities; you may pass from the stop before to the stop after when you toss heads.

4. When you land on a YELLOW space, follow the instructions.

5. Every time your turn comes, tell your partner where you are or where you are going. Discuss your partner's cities with him/her. (Talk about the weather, things to do, hotels, etc.)

Useful language

A: I'm going to visit Tokyo.
B: When I was there it was raining.
   Are you going to Mount Fuji?
   There's a good hotel near the airport.

Optional extras Units 1–4

Whenever you have extra time . . .

---

1 Share information *(Unit 1)*

Student B: Go to page 39.
Student A: You and Student B have different information about these courses.
Ask each other questions and complete the table below.

Yoga		T-Th 7:30–9 P.M.	
	Mr. (Red) Cross		North pool
Rock climbing		Sat 2–6	
	Amy Rowen	M-W-F 6–7 A.M.	
Cross-country cycling			Meet in front of the library

---

2 Concentrate! *(Unit 1)*

Student A: You have five minutes to do the tasks in the boxes. While you are trying to concentrate, Student B will ask you questions. You must answer these questions truthfully.
Student B: Try to prevent Student A from concentrating on the tasks. Ask questions such as
• What time did you get up today?
• What are you going to do this weekend?
• What color are your socks?

When five minutes are up, change roles and do the activity again.

solve this problem

$$654 \times 29$$

unscramble these words

MENBUR

HOPEN

memorize this poem

God in his wisdom
made the fly
And then forgot
to tell us why.

Ogden Nash

---

3 Share information *(Unit 2)*

Student B: Go to page 39.
Student A: You are having trouble reading the titles of some of the books on the bookshelf. Ask Student B for help. Take turns asking and answering questions.

Useful language

Where is [the dictionary]?
What book is [next to the plant]?

Find:
Garfield
Chess
Photography
How to Tell Jokes
Short Stories of
    Hemmingway
Gone with the Wind
Chinese Cooking
French Castles

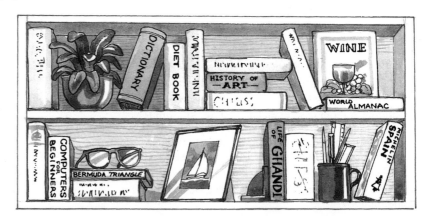

4 Conditional game (Unit 2)

4 Conversation game *(Unit 2)*

There are two conversations here. Student A begins.

Student A   Student B

1 Hello? OR
  Good afternoon. May I help you?

2 May I speak to _____, please? OR
  Could I see those sunglasses, please?

3 Here. Would you like to try them on? OR
  Speaking.

4 Are you still selling a used bicycle? OR
  Yes, I'd better. Do you have a mirror?

5 Yes, I am. Would you like to see it? OR
  There's one on the wall behind you.

6 Do you have them in a lighter color? OR
  Yes, I would. Can I go there now?

7 Certainly. Here's a pair of gray ones. OR
  Sure. I'm not doing anything now.

8 I'll take them. How much are they? OR
  And how much are you selling it for?

9 They're on sale for $15. OR
  It's almost new, so I want $100 for it.

10 OK. I'll be there in a few minutes. OR
   Do you take credit cards?

11 All right. Goodbye. OR
   Yes, we do. Here's your receipt.

---

5 Rhythm practice (Unit 3)

5 Rhythm practice *(Unit 3)*

Repeat each line. Then practice as group A and
group B.

A   **"GUS"**   **B**

He thinks he's the greatest
He thinks he's the best.

      He thinks he's the smartest
      Better than the rest.

It's true he's the tallest
The most handsome too.

      His hair is the blackest
      His eyes the brightest blue.

It's true he's the richest

      And has the fastest car.

His house is the biggest

      He lives like a star!

His name is Ferguson
But people call him Gus.

      He only has one problem
      He's not as nice as us!

---

6 Crazy stories (Unit 3)

6 Crazy stories *(Unit 3)*

Student B: Go to page 39.
Student A: Complete your part of this crazy story.
Then read the whole story aloud with Student B.

1 .... (man's name)

3 at/in .... (place)

5 When he ....

7 Then when they were ....

9 He said ....

---

7 Number practice (Unit 3)

7 Number practice *(Unit 3)*

Notice how we say these numbers. Say them
yourself.

8½	eight and a half
3.86	three point eight six
237	two hundred (and) thirty-seven
in 1887	in eighteen eighty-seven [year]
400,000,000	four hundred million [not millions]
220,000	two hundred (and) twenty thousand

Student B: Go to page 39.
Student A: Write the numbers Student B reads.
            Check your answers. Write some more
            numbers and read them to Student B,
            then check answers again.

8 Role play (Unit 4)

Student A: You are the client. Think of five things to ask the palm reader about your future.

Student B: You are the palmist. Examine Student A's hand and answer his/her questions about the future. Use the information below.

> A: I'm studying to be a doctor. Am I going to make it?
> B: Your head line shows you are practical. You are going to be a good doctor.

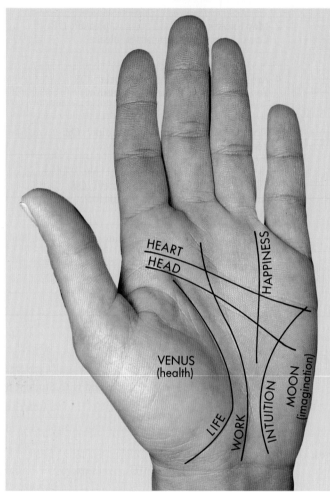

- **LIFE:**
  A very long line means a long life. A broken line indicates sickness.

- **HEART:**
  A long line shows happiness in love. A short line indicates problems.

- **HEAD:**
  A line that is high and straight indicates a practical personality. A line that curves and goes down shows creativity.

- **WORK:**
  A line that begins near the wrist and goes to the fingers means hard work and success. If the line begins at the side of the hand, it means fame.

- **INTUITION:**
  Only some people have this line. It means they know things without being told.

- **HAPPINESS:**
  If it begins at the head line, it means happiness in middle age. If it begins at the heart line, it means happiness in old age. A long line means good luck.

9 Vocabulary treasure hunt (Unit 4)

This box has some adjectives and some endings to put on adjectives to make new words. How many new words can you make in two minutes? (Make sure you can spell them.) Work with a partner.

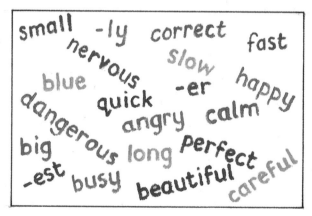

Optional extras   Units 1–4
Student B

1 Share information (page 36)

You and Student A have different information about these courses.
Ask each other questions and complete the table below.

	Sid Hatha		Music room A
Cowards' swimming		T-Th 7–8	
	Ben Nevis		Summit Park
Rowing			Beaver Lake
	Rhoda Ride	Sun mornings (leave at 8:00)	

3 Share information (page 36)

You are having trouble reading the titles of some of
the books on the bookshelf. Ask Student A for help.
Take turns asking and answering questions.

Find:
Diet Book
World Almanac
The Life of Ghandi
Computers for Beginners
Bermuda Triangle
History of Art
Wine
Michelin's Spain

Useful language:

Where is [the dictionary]?
What book is [next to the plant]?

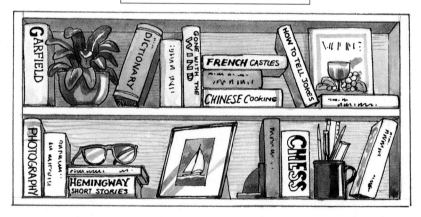

6 Crazy stories (page 37)

Make up a crazy story with Student A by completing
your part of it. Then read the whole story aloud with
Student A.

2 saw .... (woman's name)

4 at .... (time)

6 She was .... (action)

8 .... (something happened)

10 So they ....

7 Number practice (page 37)

Read these numbers to Student A. Then check your
answers.

491	in 1986	400,000
223	434.4	20,000,000
2.72	418	205,000
in 1871	800,000	199,854.

Now write the numbers Student A says to you.

Crazy Crimes

Here are five true stories about criminals who were caught in funny ways. Complete the stories and fill in the crossword on the other page with the missing words.

Smile

In Pittsburgh, Pennsylvania a man robbed the police! One of the things he stole was a .... (1 across) that took instant pictures. He didn't .... (8 across) the ...., (13 across) so he threw it .... (3 down) in a wastebasket. The .... (15 down) used the picture to .... (28 across) the thief.

My boots!

A .... (19 down) man robbed the .... (14 down) of a police officer in Detroit Michigan. The police officer .... (6 down) recognize the 18-year-old, but he .... (17 down) that he was the thief. How? It was .... (18 across) The young man was .... (25 across) the policeman's boots!

Could you spell that, please?

Another man .... (12 down) a note on a piece of .... (15 across) and used it to steal $8,000 from a .... (27 across) in Bloomfield, New Jersey. Police didn't have any .... (20 across) finding the robber, because he .... (2 down) a very stupid mistake. .... (7 across) note was written .... (9 across) the back of his salary statement . . . with his .... (10 down) on it!

A hat trick

A man from Lake Worth, Florida thought his imagination .... (4 across) playing tricks on him when he drove past a teenager one day. The boy was wearing new tennis .... (11 down) and a .... (23 down) hat. The man offered the boy a ride, and then .... (16 down) him that he needed .... (21 across) stop to buy something at a .... (5 down) Instead he .... (24 across) the police. The shoes and hat had been stolen from the man's house the day before.

Just like the movies

A bank robber in Sacramento, California decided that a dark movie theater was the perfect .... (22 down) to .... (26 down) from the police. But .... (26 across) got so .... (30 down) in the ...., (28 down) Robocop, that he didn't notice that they were asking everybody to leave the theater. They caught .... (29 across) when they turned on the lights!

Fifth unit
How long have you been a runner?

0 ⇄
Warm-up

Ask your classmates questions to find someone who does each of these things. When someone says "yes" to a question, write that person's name beside the number. How many "yes" answers did you get?

Find someone who . . .
1 . . . goes running almost every day.
2 . . . is learning to play a new sport.
3 . . . played volleyball yesterday.
4 . . . can ride a horse well.
5 . . . never watches sports on T.V.
6 . . . is on a sports team.
7 . . . went swimming yesterday.
8 . . . is trying to lose weight.
9 . . . came to class on a bicycle.
10 . . . hates to play sports.

1 🔘
Get ready

Kenji and Tex are both waiting for the elevator in the dormitory. Listen to Part 1 of their conversation. Then answer these three questions.

1 How often does Tex go running?
2 How far is Kenji planning to run?
3 What does Kenji promise Tex?

2

Dialogue: Part Two

There is an information error in each sentence. Correct it after you listen to Part 2 of the dialogue.

1 Kenji began running when he was a university student.
2 Tex suggests that they run in Lafontaine Park.
3 Tex arrived in Montreal last year.
4 Tex is studying sports medicine at McGill University.
5 Kenji speaks German well.
6 Kenji has been a doctor for thirteen years.

3

Focus on new language

Find a word or expression in the dialogue with the same meaning.

Words
1 nearer
2 cars and buses on a street
3 from another country
4 excellent, great
5 very much, to a great degree

Expressions
6 probably is
7 finished, left
8 I admire that.

Tex: How long have you been a runner?

Kenji: Oh, since I was about fifteen. How about you?

T: For a couple of years. I began when I got to college. Where are you planning to run today?

K: I was thinking about going to Lafontaine Park. Do you ever run there?

T: I *have* run there a few times, but now I usually go to Mount Royal Park. It's a lot closer, and there's less traffic on the way.

K: That sounds fine to me, just show me the way. You seem to know Montreal really well. How long have you lived here?

T: I've been here since June, but I don't actually live here. I'm only staying for the summer. I'm taking an intensive course in French at McGill. And of course I signed up for a couple of courses at the Health and Fitness Institute.

K: Your French must be improving a lot here.

T: It really is. You know, I always thought I couldn't learn foreign languages, but I'm learning a lot. I'm enjoying it, too. Do you speak any foreign languages? Besides English, I mean?

K: I studied German in college, but I've forgotten almost all of it.

T: But your *English* is super!

K: I don't think so. It should be better, because I started studying English when I was in junior high school, and I sometimes use English in my work.

T: What do you do anyway?

K: I'm a doctor at the National Institute for Sports Medicine in Osaka.

T: That must be interesting. How long have you worked there?

K: Ever since I got out of medical school. That was three years ago.

T: I'm impressed. So, Dr. Omura, is running good exercise?

K: I recommend it highly, Mr. Travis. Let's go!

4 ⇄ 📼
First practice

First, repeat each of these conversations. Then, practice it with other students.

▶ Find out someone's occupation:

A: | What do you <u>do</u>?
| What do you do for a <u>living</u>?

B: I'm a | <u>student</u> at [McGill University].
| [<u>pharmacist</u>] at [a <u>drugstore</u>].

▶ Find out the length of time at that job or school:

A: How long have you | <u>been</u> there?
| gone to <u>school</u> there?
| <u>worked</u> there?

B: Since | [<u>1987</u>].
| [<u>June</u>].
| last [<u>September</u>].
| I was in [<u>high</u> school].

▶ Find out exactly when the person began:

A: | <u>When</u> in [1987]?
| When was <u>that</u>?

B: I began | in [<u>January</u> of 1987].
| on [June <u>tenth</u>].
That was | [two <u>years</u>] ago.
| when I was [fif<u>teen</u>].

5 📼
Focus on pronunciation

Listen to these pairs of words with the /iy/ and /ɪ/ sounds, and then repeat them:

leave – live
feel – fill
reach – rich

▶ Listen to each sentence and mark the word you hear.

1 leave – live
2 feel – fill
3 reach – rich
4 he's – his
5 steal – still
6 sheep – ship

▶ Now listen to these sentences, and repeat them. Pay particular attention to the way that you pronounce the /iy/ and /ɪ/ sounds.

1 Ouch! These shoes don't fit my feet.
2 This cheese is really good. Try it!
3 Where's Jim? He's still in his seat.
4 At least give me the list.
5 She's going to leave this city.

6
Find the rule: the present perfect

Look at these sentences, and answer the questions below:

1 I came to Montreal last June.
2 I have been in Montreal since June.

Last June

| The past | June | | Now |

Since last June

- What is the verb in sentence 1?
- What is the time expression?
- Is the action finished?
- When do we use the simple past tense?
  a) for completed past actions.
  b) for actions that began in the past and continue to the present.

- What are the verb forms in sentence 2?
- What is the time expression?
- Is the situation finished?
- When do we use the present perfect tense?
  a) for completed past actions.
  b) for actions that began in the past and continue to the present.

Now apply the rule!

The verb tense in each of these sentences is wrong. Correct the verbs.

David: How long are you a student here? *have you been*
Maria: I am here since last January.
I have gone to a different school last year (but I didn't like it).
I have left that other school at the end of the semester.
D: Are you happy since you came to this school?
M: Yes. I made lots of friends since I've been here.

7
Transfer

Talk with another student about your English class.

Student A **Student B**

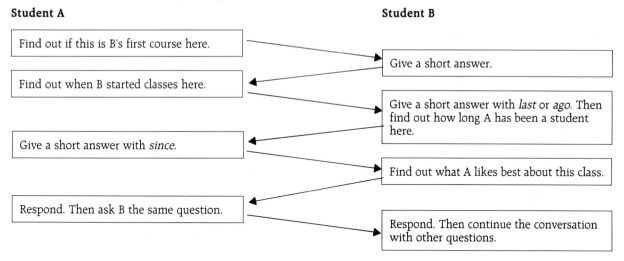

Student A	Student B
Find out if this is B's first course here.	
	Give a short answer.
Find out when B started classes here.	
	Give a short answer with *last* or *ago*. Then find out how long A has been a student here.
Give a short answer with *since*.	
	Find out what A likes best about this class.
Respond. Then ask B the same question.	
	Respond. Then continue the conversation with other questions.

8
Share information

Student A: How much do you know about the characters in our book? You have some information, and Student B has other information. Ask and answer questions until you complete this table.

Student B: Go to page 49.

Useful language

What does [Kenji] do? He's a doctor.
Where does [he] work?
At [the National Institute of Sports Medicine].
How long has [he] worked/been there?
[He's] worked/been there since [1987].

Name	Occupation	Place of work or study	There since . . .
Kenji	doctor		1987
Jean		Women at Large	
Heather	grade school student		1990
Tex		University of Texas	
Marta	college student		1988
Diane		East End Senior Citizens' Centre	
Yves	lawyer		1985

Run for your life!

"Anything wrong?"

Since the mid-1960s, millions of people in the United States and in other countries have been jogging three or more times a week. Jogging has become
5 popular because it is healthy and easy to do. All you need is comfortable running shoes and a place to run. What is jogging anyway? Basically, jogging is just a form of running. But joggers are not usually

10 interested in how fast they run; they do it for exercise, not to win races.

Jogging is good exercise when it is done regularly: at least three times a week. It strengthens the leg muscles,
15 and, because it forces the heart to beat faster, it also improves blood circulation. Many people also jog to help control their weight. Joggers burn up 62 calories for every kilometer they run. In addition,
20 jogging helps decrease levels of emotional stress.

Jogging can also help you live longer. A scientific study published recently in the *New England Journal of Medicine*
25 states that a regular program of moderate exercise can add as much as two years to a person's life. Almost 17,000 graduates of Harvard University participated in the study between the mid-1970s and 1978.
30 Men who burned up at least 2,000 calories a week by exercising lived longer on the average than men who did not exercise. That means that more men who didn't exercise died during those years
35 than men who did exercise: 25% more, to be specific.

Fortunately you can burn up 2,000 calories with just a few hours of exercise a week. For example, five hours of fast
40 walking, four hours of jogging, or three hours of playing squash each use about 2,000 calories. So all you need to do is walk for an hour five times a week, or jog for 30 to 40 minutes every day, or play
45 squash three times a week for an hour to get into, and stay in, good shape.

Then why don't more people get enough exercise? The main problems are first, finding enough time to exercise,
50 and then, not giving up once you get started. So if you want to stay healthy and live longer, put on your running shoes and go jogging. And remember that shoes, a pair of shorts and a t-shirt
55 don't take up much space in your suitcase when you go away for a weekend or on vacation.

Read on your own

9 ⇄
Warm-up

What do you think of runners? First, choose five adjectives that come to your mind when you think of people who run. Then, work with one or two other students and compare the adjectives each of you chose. Give reasons for your choices. Finally, try to make one list of five adjectives that all of you agree on.

attractive	boring	calm	crazy	desperate
friendly	fun	healthy	independent	intelligent
practical	quiet	relaxed	ridiculous	selfish
sensible	strong	stupid	vain	worried

10
Specific information

Read the article "Run for your life," and classify these statements as T (true) or F (false).

1 Jogging has been popular in the U.S. for over 25 years.
2 Jogging is slower than regular running, and it is non-competitive.
3 Jogging makes people feel more tense and nervous.
4 The amount of exercise a person gets does not influence the age he or she will live to be.
5 People who don't like to run can burn up just as many calories a week by doing other activities.
6 It is impossible for people to get enough exercise when they travel.

11
Focus on words

Fill in the table with verbs and nouns from the article.

Verbs	Nouns
circulate	*circulation*
add	
....	statement
live	
....	death
....	exercise

12
Vocabulary in context

Match the underlined words in these sentences with the definitions to the right.

a) luckily
b) consume, use
c) lower, diminish
d) in general
e) makes stronger
f) stopping, quitting

...... 1 It strengthens the leg muscles ... (line 14)
...... 2 Joggers burn up 62 calories for every kilometer they run. (line 18)
...... 3 ... jogging helps decrease levels of emotional stress. (line 20)
...... 4 Men who burned up at least 2,000 calories a week lived longer on the average than men who did not exercise. (line 30)
...... 5 Fortunately you can burn up 2,000 calories with just a few hours of exercise. (line 37)
...... 6 The main problems are first, finding enough time to exercise, and then, not giving up once you get started. (line 48)

13 ⇄
Role play

Student A: Imagine that you are talking to a friend about a problem. For example, maybe you are too heavy or too thin, you have a very high level of stress, or you are always tired. You are very busy, so you don't have much time to exercise.

Student B: Listen to Student A's problems, and then suggest some solutions. For example, maybe A should start jogging or doing some sport like tennis, squash or swimming. Or why doesn't A start walking to work or school? Try to convince A of the benefits of exercise. Give reasons for your suggestions.

14
Laugh and learn

Look at this Garfield cartoon.
How long has Garfield been "human"? That is, how long has he *pretended* to be human?
Try to retell what happened in the cartoon. Say at least one sentence about each picture. For example:
Garfield was walking down the street one day when he noticed a bakery.

> **Vocabulary notes:**
>
> **bakery** = a place to buy cakes, donuts, and other sweet things to eat
> **allowed** = permitted
> **roots** = literally, the part of a plant that is under the ground. Here, it means one's origins.

1. GARFIELD

After "since" we use a time expression that indicates a point in time.
For example: *How long have you been here?*
Since 3 o'clock/June 18th/1989/last night.

► Notice that Garfield says that he has been human *for ten minutes now.*
What does the time expression *for ten minutes* indicate?   a) a point in time.
                                                              b) a period of time.

► Make two lists: one with time expressions that we use after *for*,
and another list with the time expressions that we use after *since*.

... June	... a long time
... two months	... several hours
... an hour	... this morning
... last year	... three years
... 1988	... 8:30
... yesterday	... I was born

> **for + periods of time**
>
> *two months*
>
> **since + points in time**
>
> *June*

15 🔘
Live from CWHF

The Johnny Carton Show is on the radio now, and we're just in time for a commercial from Johnny's sponsor, the Magic Vitamin Company. Before you listen to the commercial, read the questions under the pictures.

1 Why was Mr. Klutz late for his first appointment?
2 Why couldn't the nurse ask him any questions?

3 What problem did Mr. Klutz tell the doctor about?
4 How long has he felt that way?
5 What was Dr. Feelgood's diagnosis?

6 How does Mr. Klutz look when he comes back a month later?
7 How does he get to work now?
8 What ingredient is in Magic Vitamins?

▶ **Role play**
Work in groups of three and do a "live" presentation of this commercial.
Try to remember some of the lines from the commercial, but feel free to use your own words too.

Student B

8 Share information (page 45)

You have some information about the characters in our book, and Student A has other information. Work with Student A, asking and answering questions until you complete the table.

> **Useful language**
>
> What does [Kenji] do? He's a doctor.
> Where does [he] work?
> At [the National Institute of Sports Medicine].
> How long has [he] worked/been there?
> [He's] worked/been there since [1987].

Name	Occupation	Place of work or study	There since . . .
Kenji		National Institute of Sports Medicine	
Jean	owner and manager		1984
Heather		Lakeview Middle School	
Tex	university student		1988
Marta		University of São Paulo	
Diane	physical therapist		1989
Yves		Ogilvy Associates	

Sixth unit
Would you mind not smoking?

0 ⮂
Warm-up

How would you react? How do you
feel about people who do these
things? Talk to a classmate and make
a list of several possible solutions for
each situation.

1 Someone talks during a movie.
2 Someone gets in line in front of you
at the bank.
3 Someone has a long conversation
on a public phone while you wait
for your turn.
4 Someone calls you several times
very late at night, but it is the
wrong number.
5 Someone starts smoking in a "no
smoking" area of an airplane or a
restaurant.

1 🎞
Get ready

Diane, Marta, and Jean are watching
T.V. when the doorbell rings. Diane
lets Tex and Kenji in. Listen to Part 1
of their conversation. Then answer
these three questions.

1 How does Jean feel about flying?
2 What food is making people sick?
3 What does Jean want to order?

Jean: That was good. I really enjoyed eating pizza for a change. Coffee for everybody?

Diane: I know what you mean. Marta really dislikes having "junk food" around. She keeps reminding us about good nutrition. Don't you, Marta?

Marta: And about drinking too much coffee.

Kenji: She's right, you know. Staying healthy takes a lot of work and, how do you say it?

M: Willpower.

K: That's it, willpower. Do you have an ashtray by any chance?

J: No, we don't!

D: Kenji, would you mind not smoking?

K: Oh ... Of course not. Sorry, I didn't know ...

D: You're in a "no smoking" home. In fact, I just quit smoking a couple of weeks ago. But I have to admit, sometimes I miss having a cigarette with my coffee.

K: That's my problem, too. I guess it's just one of my weaknesses. I ought to try to quit.

J: I didn't mean to be rude, Kenji, but *we* all appreciate breathing clean air.

K: That's O.K. I understand. Diane, how did you do it? I mean give up smoking?

D: Actually, Jean convinced me.

J: I did? I don't even remember talking to you about it!

D: You didn't talk – you wrote. Remember when you were looking for roommates? Your notice said, "Quiet, non-smokers only."

J: You mean you gave up smoking so you could share the apartment?

D: Exactly. I finished reading the notice, and then threw away my cigarettes.

K: Just like that? Was it that easy?

D: I didn't say *that*. The hard part is that I get hungry all the time. Jean is anti-smoking and Marta is anti-junk food! You can't win.

2

Dialogue: Part Two

Listen to Part 2 of the dialogue. Then write **That's right**, **That's wrong**, or **I don't know** for each sentence.

1 Marta likes healthy food.
2 Jean gives Kenji an ashtray.
3 Kenji plans to give up smoking.
4 Diane doesn't smoke anymore.
5 Jean asked Diane to quit smoking.
6 Jean has never smoked.

3

Focus on new language

Find a word or expression in the dialogue with the same meaning.

Words
1 determination
2 place to put cigarette ashes
3 feel the absence of
4 deficiencies, faults

Expressions
5 two
6 should
7 stop
8 got rid of

4

First practice

First, repeat each of these conversations. Then, practice it with other students.

▶ Ask someone to stop doing something:

    A: Would you mind not | talking?
                             | smoking?
                             | calling after 11?

      B: | Sorry.
         | Of course not.

▶ Explain your request:

    A: | I'm watching the news.
      | You're in the "no-smoking" section.
      | Everybody's asleep then.

      B: I guess I can | wait.
                  | go somewhere else.
                  | phone again tomorrow.

▶ Apologize:

    A: I didn't mean to be rude, but I
       | enjoy watching the news.
       | dislike breathing smoky air.
       | appreciate getting to bed early.

      B: | That's O.K.
         | No problem.
         | I understand.

5

Find the rule: verbs followed by gerund (V + *ing*) objects

Go back to the dialogue on page 51. Read it again.
Make a list of all the verbs that are followed by a gerund object.

	verb	gerund		verb	gerund
line 1	....	....	line 24	....	....
line 5	....	....	line 30	....	....
line 6	....	....	line 33	....	....
line 18	....	....	line 36	....	....
line 22	....	....	line 44	....	....

Now apply the rule!

Put one of the verbs from your list in each blank to complete the conversation. Do not use the same verb twice.

Paul: Would you .....*main*..... closing the window and turning on the air conditioner? It's a little warm in here.

Marie: Sorry, the air conditioner is broken.

Paul: What? Again? They just ...*finished*... fixing it last week.

Marie: Yeah, I know. But to tell you the truth, I .... having that cold air blowing on me. Actually, I .... having the window open for a change.

Paul: Well, I .... working in a cool office.

Marie: I know what we should do. We should .... complaining, leave early today, and go relax in the park for the rest of the afternoon.

I didn't mean to be rud
I didn't mean to bother you
I didn't mean to worrie you
I didn't mean to hurt you .

6 ⇄
Transfer

Make polite requests. For example, ask B to stop doing something, ask to borrow something, or ask for a favor. Change roles and practice again.

Useful language	**A**	**Functions**	**B**	*Useful language*
Would you mind turning the music down? not playing the music so loud?	Ask someone (not) to do something.			
		Agree to do what A asks.		Of course not. Sure.
I'm trying to study. I want to make a phone call.	Explain your request – give a reason for it.			
		Apologize.		Sorry. I didn't mean to bother you. Oh. I didn't know.
Thanks. I didn't mean to be rude, but I need to finish reading this. dislike talking on the phone when there's a lot of noise around.	Thank B, and soften your tone.			
		Accept A's reasons.		That's O.K. I understand.

7
Focus on pronunciation

Listen to how these words end. Then answer the questions:

thin	think	thing
ban	bank	bang

- Do any of the words in each group end with the same sound?
- Which words end with an "n" sound?
- Which words end with a "k" sound?
- Do any words end with a "g" sound?

▶ Listen to each sentence and circle the word you hear.

1 thin   think
2 in   ink
3 sun   sung
4 ran   rang
5 bring   brink

▶ In a conversation, words ending in *-ing* sometimes sound like they end in "in":
Susana is walking in the park.
Susana likes to walk in the park.

Listen to each sentence and circle the words you hear.
6 dancing   dance in
7 taking   take in
8 coming   come in
9 getting   get in

▶ Now rewind the tape and repeat each sentence.

8 ⇄
Role play

Student B: Go to page 57.
Student A: You are in a bookstore.

- You want to buy a book to read on a long plane trip. But you don't know exactly what you want.
- You just finished reading a good mystery, and you enjoyed it.
- You don't like spy books. You even dislike looking at the covers.
- You enjoy reading Agatha Christie books, but you never remember which ones you've read.
- You keep trying to read science fiction, but you never finish the book.

Ask the clerk (Student B) for help.
Here are some other kinds of books. Decide on something to buy. (Consider buying magazines or newspapers if you give up buying a book.)

Biography	Fantasy
Western	Adventure
Romance	Terror

SMOKERS NEED NOT APPLY

The United States is now becoming a non-smoking society. Across the country, hundreds of towns and cities, and even entire states, are making strict laws to control the sale and use of cigarettes. In New York, for example, smoking is illegal in public buildings, hospitals, schools, banks, stores, movie theaters, taxi-cabs, and restrooms, to name a few places. In addition, smoking is prohibited anywhere in the U.S. on airline flights that last two hours or less. And now many private companies have also made rules about cigarette smoking. At least 40% of American companies restrict smoking by their employees.

Company policies are mostly of three kinds: they prohibit smoking by employees when they are working, they hire only non-smokers, or they force workers who smoke to quit smoking. The first type of policy tries to ban smoking, but the other two go further; they ban the smokers, too.

Restrictions on smoking in the workplace are meant to provide a smoke-free work environment – especially for non-smokers. Recent research has shown that non-smokers who breathe air containing cigarette smoke may develop lung cancer and other serious diseases. According to statistics, 75% of Americans think that people should smoke only in private. And at Texas Instruments, the calculator manufacturer, 90% of the employees support the company's policies to protect non-smokers.

Companies that refuse to employ smokers are thinking of more than their workers' health. There are also important economic reasons behind their policies. Employees who smoke get sick and miss work more often than non-smokers. They also have more accidents and get less work done. Companies hope to save money and improve workers' health by forcing employees to quit smoking.

Fortunately, most employees agree. Some surveys show that up to 50 million of the 55 million American smokers have tried to quit smoking at least once. One smoker trying to give up cigarettes said, "A lot of smokers secretly hope their employers ban smoking to help them quit."

Read on your own

9 ⇄
Warm-up

Some companies require their
employees to wear special types of
clothing or have specific skills.
Sometimes there are other
requirements. Work with a classmate
to make a list of at least five
professions, and decide what
requirements are reasonable for the
job.

> **appearance:** clothing, uniform, beard, etc.
> **skills:** computer, drive, languages, etc.
> **schedule:** weekends, evenings, overtime
> **personal:** married/single, non-smoker
> **other:** age, sex, nationality, religion

10
Main ideas

Read the article "Smokers need not
apply" and classify these statements
as T (true) or F (false).

1 People in the U.S. can smoke when and where they want.
2 American companies have made their own rules, in addition to public laws.
3 Cigarette smoking harms only the smoker, not the people nearby.
4 Companies can save money by hiring only non-smokers.
5 Most employees would prefer to quit their jobs than to quit smoking.

11
Focus on words

In the article, the word "not" is never
used to make ideas negative. But there
are many negative words in the
article. Here are some of them. Find
them in the article and match each
one to its opposite. Match nouns with
nouns; verbs with verbs; adjectives
with adjectives.

1 illegal (line 7)   .... freedom
2 prohibit (line 18)   .... allow
3 non-smokers (line 20)   ..2.. permit
4 ban (line 22)   .... legal
5 restriction (line 25)   .... agree
6 refuse (line 38)   .... smokers

12
Scanning for information

There are several numbers in this
article. As quickly as you can, find
these numbers and what they refer to.
Write the numbers in the spaces
provided. Do not try to re-read the
article; you will work faster by just
looking for the numbers. They are not
listed in the order they appear in the
article.

> 50 million   90%   40%   55 million   75%

1 American companies that restrict smoking ....
2 Americans who think that smoking should only be done in private
  ....
3 Employees in one company who support its smoking policies ....
4 Americans who have tried to quit smoking ....
5 Americans who smoke ....

13 ⇄
Role play

Student A: Imagine that you want to hire someone to be a tour guide. Decide
           what the qualifications and requirements are, and explain them to
           the person applying for the job. For example, does the employee
           have to wear certain clothes or have certain skills? Are there age,
           sex, smoking restrictions? Does the person have to work nights or
           weekends to take tourists sightseeing?
Student B: Imagine you are applying for a job as a tour guide. Discuss the
           qualifications and requirements with the employer. Do you accept
           the requirements? Give your reasons.

14
Laugh and learn

These cartoons show you two ways of agreeing with negative statements.

▶ Look at the first cartoon. Both sentences are negative. What words make them negative?

▶ Now look at the second cartoon. There are two negative statements in it, too. What are they?

▶ For both of these cartoons, there is another way to say the second negative sentence. Compare the two ways:

And <u>neither do</u> I.
And I <u>don't either</u>.

I <u>can't</u> decide <u>either</u>.
<u>Neither can</u> I (decide).

1. GARFIELD

2. BLONDIE

Subject	Aux	Negative	(Verb)	Other
I	do	n't	X	either
I	can	't	decide	either

Negative	Aux	Subject
Neither	do	I
Neither	can	I

▶ The auxiliary comes before the subject in which sentence?
 a) the sentence with "neither".   b) the sentence with "Auxiliary + not".
▶ Where does "neither" come in a sentence?
 a) at the beginning, before the auxiliary.   b) at the end.
▶ Where does "either" come in a sentence?
 a) at the beginning, before the auxiliary.   b) at the end.
▶ Sentences with "not . . . either" and "neither"
 a) agree.   b) disagree.

Now apply the rule!
Agree with these negative statements.

1 A: I didn't finish watching the movie.

 B: I didn't ....

2 A: I don't mind sharing a room.

 B: .... do I.

3 A: I can't stand waiting in line.

 B: Neither ....

4 A: I don't enjoy long flights.

 B: .... either.

5 A: I don't remember asking Ann to come.

 B: ....

15 📼
Live from CWHF

CWHF has a call-in program for listeners to call the radio station and give their opinions. The calls are broadcast live so that others can listen to them.

▶ Listen to today's program and answer these questions.

   1 What is the topic of the program?
   2 One caller makes impolite comments. Which one?
   3 Jean is one of the callers. Which one?

▶ Can you remember which caller said each sentence? Write 1, 2 or 3 next to each one. Then listen again to check your answers.

   .... "They are basically unhappy."
   .... "They're very nice, always in a good mood."
   .... "The problem these people have is with their self-image."
   .... "Sometimes I wonder how they can tie their shoes."
   .... "I run a fitness center for heavy women."
   .... "It's not their fault."

▶ Which of the callers do you think would say these things? Explain why.

   .... I think the whole idea is just a joke.
   .... I think they need a lot of sympathy.
   .... I think we have to develop self-confidence.

Student B

8 Role play *(page 53)*

You are the sales clerk in a bookstore. A customer is asking for your help. These are the kinds of books you can recommend:

- There is a new spy thriller out. Everybody is buying it.
- Your store has a very good selection of science fiction.
- Many people like to read books by Agatha Christie, just to pass the time.
- Your store also has other types of books such as biography, western, romance, fantasy, terror, adventure.
- You can offer Student A some other kind of reading material such as newspapers and magazines, or puzzle books.

Make sure that Student A doesn't leave the store without buying something.

Seventh unit How do you do it?

0 ⇄
Warm-up

Think of some simple activity you can do almost without thinking. It might be something like tying a shoelace. Is it easy to explain how to do it? Talk about this with one or two classmates and make a list of the steps needed to do one of these activities, or one you think of yourself.

- drawing a star with five points
- tying a shoelace
- riding a bicycle
- shifting gears in a car
- putting on a tie

1 ▭
Get ready

Marta sees Kenji sitting on the grass in front of the dormitory on the McGill campus one afternoon. Listen to Part 1 of their conversation. Then answer these three questions.

1 Where did Marta just come from?
2 What is Kenji eating?
3 What does Marta have for lunch?

2 🔊
Dialogue: Part Two

There is an information error in each sentence. Correct it after you listen to Part 2 of the dialogue.

1 Kenji usually eats in his room at the dorm.
2 Marta has never been to a Japanese restaurant.
3 Marta thinks it is hard to eat rice with chopsticks.
4 Kenji tells Marta how to make noodles.
5 Marta wants to go to the restaurant alone.
6 Kenji is going to call Marta in a couple of days.

3
Focus on new language

Find a word or expression in the dialogue with the same meaning.

Words
1 self-service restaurant
2 string-like food made of eggs and flour

Expressions
3 lift something
4 reverse it
5 choose something
6 discuss it
7 telephone you
8 as a precaution

Marta: Do you always have Japanese food for lunch?

Kenji: Not always. Usually I eat at the cafeteria in the dorm. Do you like Japanese food?

M: Some of it. There are a lot of Japanese restaurants in São Paulo, you know. And I've gone to a few of them.

K: What do you like best?

M: Well, I guess I like "yakisoba" best, but noodles are *so hard* to eat with chopsticks. I don't know how you can do it so easily.

K: Maybe you don't hold them correctly. Would you like me to show you how to use them?

M: Sure.

K: O.K. First you pick up one chopstick, like this.

M: Like this?

K: No, hold it like you hold a pencil. And turn it around; it's upside down.

M: Oh, O.K. Now what?

K: Then you put the other one where your thumb meets your hand, and rest it on your third finger.

M: All right. But how do you *move* them?

K: Only the top one moves. You just hold them up, and pick up the food. It's not so hard once you get used to it.

M: Probably not, if you grow up doing it!

K: Really all you need is practice. There are a couple of Japanese restaurants you could go to not far from here.

M: Maybe we could all go. You too Kenji. And you could help us pick out what to order. What do you think?

K: It's fine with me.

M: O.K. then. I'll talk it over with Diane and Jean, and Yves, of course. Can you ask Tex if he wants to go too?

K: I'd be glad to.

M: Terrific. I'll call you up in a couple of days, O.K.? But *I'm* going to eat *before* we go to the restaurant, just in case the chopsticks don't work.

4 ⤨ 📼
First practice

First, repeat each of these conversations. Then, practice it with other students.

▶ Ask someone what they're doing:

A: | What're you <u>doing</u>?
 | What's that you're <u>doing</u>?
B: I'm trying to figure out how to [use this <u>video</u> recorder].

▶ Offer help:

A: | Would you like me to show you how to <u>do</u> it?
 | Maybe I can <u>help</u>.
B: | <u>Sure</u>.
 | That would be <u>great</u>.

▶ Give step-by-step instructions:

A: | First you [turn it <u>on</u>], like <u>this</u>.
 | First [push the "<u>power</u>" button.]
B: | <u>O.K.</u>. <u>Then</u> what?
 | Like <u>this</u>?
A: | Then you [put in the <u>tape</u>].
 | Then you [rewind the <u>tape</u>].
B: <u>All</u> right/Oh, <u>O</u>.K.

▶ Reassure the person:

A: | It's not so hard once you get <u>used</u> to it.
 | All you need is <u>practice</u>.
B: | You're probably <u>right</u>.
 | Thanks for your <u>help</u>.

5
Find the rule: two-word verbs

Many verbs in English come in two parts. Look at these sentences using one type of two-word verb.

Pick up the pencils.   Call up Marta.
Pick them up.   Call her up.

Wake up Tex.   Throw away the paper.
Wake him up.   Throw it away.

▶ Underline the two parts of the verb in the examples.

▶ Where does a pronoun belong with this type of two-word verb?
  a) after the verb.
  b) between the two parts of the verb.

Now apply the rule!

Here are some other two-word verbs like the ones in the examples.
Match them with their meanings. Then complete the conversations using them.
Write one word in each blank.

1 look (something) up   (a) donate (something)
2 try (something) on   (b) make sense of (something); understand
3 figure (something) out   (c) find (something) in a book
4 give (something) away   (d) test the fit (of something)

1 A: Look at these great sunglasses. Do you think I should buy them?

  B: I don't know. .... so I can see how they look on you.

2 A: What are you going to do with the books in this box?

  B: I'm going to .... I don't need them anymore.

3 A: Can you understand what this note says?

  B: No. The handwriting is terrible. I can't ....

4 A: Do you have the phone number of Canadian Airlines?

  B: Yes, I do. Let me .... in my address book.

6
Role play

Student A: You want to learn how to do one of these activities. Ask Student B to tell you.

> **Activities:**
>
> | | |
> |---|---|
> | get ready to dive into a pool | change the time and date on a digital watch |
> | serve a volleyball | sew a button on a shirt |
> | get on a horse | fold a paper airplane |

Student B: Explain how to do what Student A asks you about. Make sure that he/she is doing it correctly.

> **Useful language**
>
> | | |
> |---|---|
> | bend your knees/elbow/etc. | lift (something) up |
> | push (something) in | hold (something) down |
> | swing your arm/leg/etc. | put your left/right foot/hand/etc. up/down/back |

7
Focus on pronunciation

Two-word verbs are pronounced in a characteristic way. Listen to these examples. Then answer the questions:

I have to <u>talk</u> to him.
Why don't you <u>call</u> him <u>up</u> tonight?

What do you <u>think</u> about the movie?
I can't <u>figure</u> it <u>out</u>.

I don't know what to <u>say</u> to them.
You should <u>write</u> it <u>down</u> first.

▶ The first sentence in each example has a single word verb. Which word in these sentences has the most stress?
  a) the verb itself.
  b) the preposition after the verb.

▶ The second sentence in each example has a two word verb. Which word in these sentences has the most stress?
  a) the first part of the verb.
  b) the second part of the verb.

▶ Now look at these sentences and underline the word that is said with the most stress. Then listen to the tape to check your answers.

  1 I'm going to look it up.
  2 When did you write to her?
  3 When you're finished put it away.
  4 Could you help me put this together?
  5 Are you going to go with them?
  6 What time should I wake you up?

▶ Now rewind the tape and repeat the sentences.

8
Share information

Anna, Barbara, Carla and Diana share an apartment. One morning one of them turned on the toaster and forgot to turn it off. At 7:15 the smell of burned toast filled the apartment, and the toaster was ruined. Ask your partner questions to fill in the table, and figure out which woman should buy a new toaster.
Student B: Go to page 65.

Name	Breakfast	Time ate	Other activity
Anna			Got up at 7:15 and woke Barbara
Diana		×	Took a shower from 7:10 to 7:20
Carla	Coffee and toast	6:30	
Barbara	Orange juice		

FOUR DISCOVERIES THAT CHANGED MEDICINE

Over 200 years ago, a well-known English scientist and doctor, Dr. William Withering, saw the "miraculous" recovery of several patients who suffered from a deadly heart disease. He asked them how they were cured and was told that a good "witch" who lived nearby had given them a special tea made of plants. After talking to the woman healer and testing the many ingredients she used in her remedy, Dr. Withering identified the most powerful plant. Digitalis is the name of the drug made from this plant. It is probably one of the most important natural products discovered for medical use. Digitalis has been used since the 1770s to save the lives of people with heart disease.

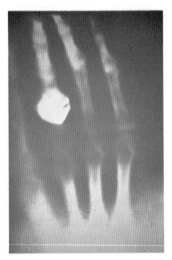

Konrad Roentgen, a German scientist, was experimenting with light when he came across a new type of lightwave he had never seen before. He knew it was some kind of ray, but he didn't understand it. Because of this, he gave it the name "x (unknown) ray". Roentgen wanted to find out about the properties of this new light, x-ray, so he began by trying to use it in photography. On December 22, 1895, he took a picture of his wife's hand. When the film was developed, Roentgen was very surprised at what he saw. Instead of a picture of his wife's hand, he had a picture of the bones of her hand, with her ring on one finger. Today x-rays are one of the most important methods we have to examine bone disorders.

The discovery of the antibiotic penicillin was announced in 1928 by Dr. Alexander Fleming. Dr. Fleming found the mold (a kind of fungus) that produces it growing in one of the dishes he was using to study bacteria. After looking carefully at the dish, he found that there were no more bacteria in it. The mold had fallen there by accident, but Fleming quickly guessed that it had killed the bacteria. Dr. Fleming put some of the mold into other dishes of bacteria, and the same thing happened. A medication, the "miracle drug" penicillin, was developed from this mold. It is used to cure infections and has saved many lives. Dr. Alexander Fleming won a Nobel Prize for this important contribution to medicine.

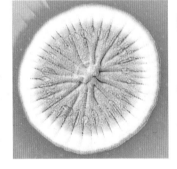

What is the frogs' secret? They live in water containing all kinds of germs, but the injuries they receive get better quickly with no infection. Dr. Michael Zasloff, a researcher at the Institute for Child Health and Human Development in the U.S., wanted to find out what kind of protection frogs have that humans don't have. He thought about the largest protective part of all animals, the skin, and decided to look into the composition of frogs' skin. Dr. Zasloff found out that frogs have two very important chemicals in their skin which act as natural antibiotics against infection. These chemicals are called "magainins." Magainins were discovered only in 1987, and nobody knows yet how they will be used in medicine. But they will probably bring about important changes.

Read on your own

9 ⇄
Warm-up

What important medical discoveries do you know about? Discuss this with two or three other students in a group, and make a list of four discoveries that you think changed medicine. Then read the article to see if any of the discoveries mentioned in it are on your list.

10
Main ideas

Read the article "Four discoveries that changed medicine." Pay attention to the title: it is very objective because the article is about science. What would be the best sub-title for each of the four paragraphs? Select one that is both specific enough to state the topic clearly, and also general enough to summarize it. And remember that it should be objective.

PARAGRAPH 1   a) Digitalis   b) Drugs made from plants
                c) The witch's remedy

PARAGRAPH 2   a) Special photography   b) Roentgen's light
                c) X-rays

PARAGRAPH 3   a) Mold and bacteria   b) Antibiotics
                c) Penicillin

PARAGRAPH 4   a) Frogs' skin   b) Magainins
                c) Hope for the future

11
Summarizing: making a table

Read the article again and fill in the table. This is one way to make a summary.

Discovery	Discoverer	Date	Used for

12
Focus on words

These words are all from the article. Cross out the word in each group that doesn't belong.

1 drug, medication, infection, antibiotic
2 happened, identified, found out, discovered
3 digitalis, magainins, penicillin, bacteria
4 researcher, patient, scientist, doctor
5 testing, experimenting, trying, containing
6 injury, disorder, cure, disease

13 ⇄
Talk it over

Discuss these questions in groups of three or four.

1 Which of these conditions do you think Magainins might someday be able to cure?   sunburn
baldness
eye infections
headaches
muscle strain
food allergies
insect bites

2 If medication with magainins came as injections, pills, and creams, which do you think would be best for the conditions you chose in question one?

14
Laugh and learn

You already know how to use verbs in the present continuous and the past continuous. But do you know that some verbs in English are not used in the continuous?

Vocabulary notes:

faun = imaginary creature; half human, half animal.
beagle = the kind of dog Snoopy is.

1. PEANUTS

2 BLONDIE

► When are the children in the first cartoon *listening* to the music?
  a) now   b) always

► When does Blondie *hear* a noise in the second cartoon?
  a) now   b) always

► Which verb shows that you are *actively* paying attention (an ACTIVE verb)?
  a) "listen" b) "hear"

► Which verb *states* that you notice sound around you (a STATIVE verb)?
  a) "listen" b) "hear"

Now apply the rule!

Match the verbs that are not usually used in the continuous with the verbs that have a related meaning but that can be used in the continuous.

Stative verbs: not continuous	Active verbs: may be continuous
see	listen
hear	learn
like	look
know	get
have	enjoy

Select two of the pairs and write sentences of your own using the four verbs. Use the progressive if you can.

15 📼
Live from CWHF

In this program Marie Dubonnet is substituting for a colleague who is sick at home with a cold virus. Part of her program is called "News Chat," and in it she tells us about a new kind of virus – a computer virus.

▶ Before you listen, make a list of the questions you think Marie will answer during the "News Chat" program. For example: What is a computer virus, and who gets it?

▶ Now listen to the program on tape, and see how many of the questions on your list Marie answers. Write down these answers.

▶ How much can you remember of what Marie said about these details? Write your answers. Then listen again, and take notes to complete them. Compare your notes with your classmates.

- what a computer virus does
- where it comes from
- how to "cure" it
- an example of a computer virus – city it started in and what it did

Student B

8 Share information *(page 61)*

Name	Breakfast	Time ate	Other activity
Anna	cereal and milk	7:30	
Diana	none		
Carla			Went out to jog at 6:45. Came back at 7:15
Barbara		7:45	Helped Diana clean up the mess in the kitchen at 7:30

Eighth unit
Have you ever been to Vermont?

0
Warm-up

Talk about these questions with your classmates. Find at least one classmate who likes to do the same things as you do.

- What time of the year do you need a break?
- What do you like to do to relax at that time?
- Where do you like to go when you have a free weekend?
- How long does it take to go to a quiet place that you enjoy?
- What do you do there?

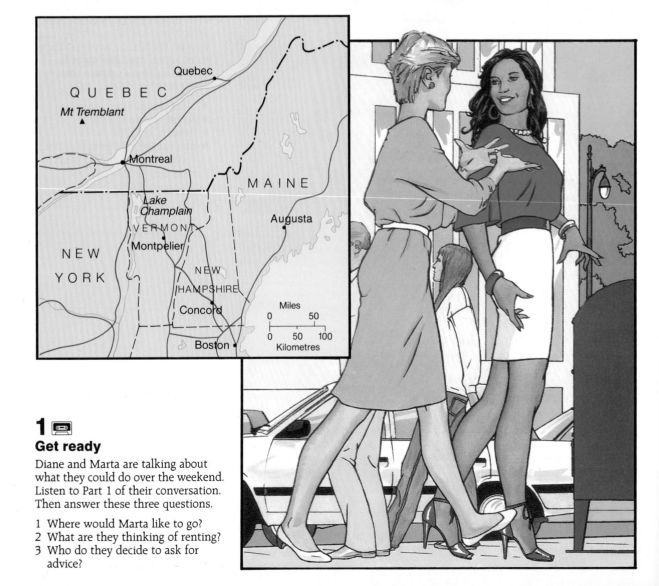

1
Get ready

Diane and Marta are talking about what they could do over the weekend. Listen to Part 1 of their conversation. Then answer these three questions.

1 Where would Marta like to go?
2 What are they thinking of renting?
3 Who do they decide to ask for advice?

Jean: Did I hear my name mentioned? Are you two gossiping about me?

Marta: Yeah, I guess you could say that . . . if you think asking for advice is "gossip."

J: What's the matter? Problems with your love life? Go ahead! I'm listening.

Diane: Oh, Jean! You're always joking! Actually, Marta and I are thinking of renting a car to go someplace peaceful to relax for the weekend. Do you have any suggestions?

J: Hmm . . . Have you ever been to Vermont?

M: The only place I've ever been in the United States is Miami.

D: I've never been there either. What's Vermont like?

J: Oh, it's beautiful! It's mostly mountains – they call them the "Green Mountains" – and forest. And there's a big lake near the border with Canada: Lake Champlain.

M: And where in Vermont should we go? To the mountains or to the lake?

J: It's probably a good idea to stay near Lake Champlain.

D: Why do you say that?

J: Because you can swim, go sailing, go waterskiing . . . and you can rent a cabin to sleep in.

D: Is it far?

J: Not at all! In fact, it probably only takes a couple of hours to drive there.

M: Really? That's fantastic. That means we could leave Friday afternoon and come back Sunday night.

D: O.K. That's settled. We're going to Vermont. Now we need to get a car, and make reservations for two nights in a cabin.

J: Why rent a car? Just take mine.

D: What if you need it?

J: I'm not doing anything special this weekend – I can always take the subway, you know.

M: Well, O.K. We'll take your car, but only if . . .

J: *If* what?

M: If *you'll* come with us.

J: Since you *insist* . . . Let's get on the phone and make our reservations!

2 🔲
Dialogue: Part Two

Listen to Part 2 of the dialogue. Then write **That's right, That's wrong**, or **I don't know** for each sentence.

1 Marta has never been to the United States.
2 Lake Champlain is in Vermont.
3 Jean likes to go to Vermont to ski.
4 Vermont is too far away to go for a weekend.
5 Jean needs to use her car in Montreal during the weekend.
6 Heather is going to Vermont with Diane and Marta.

3
Focus on new language

Find a word in the dialogue with the same meaning.

1 saying unkind things about other people
2 saying things to make people laugh
3 quiet, tranquil
4 at some time; reverse of "never"
5 dividing line between two countries
6 small house, made very simply
7 decided
8 on the condition that

4

First practice

First, repeat each of these conversations. Then, practice it with other students.

Explain what you want, and ask for advice:

► A: I'm thinking of [going out for <u>dinn</u>er].
    Do you have any sug<u>gest</u>ions?
  B: Have you ever been to [<u>Sun</u>tory]?

► Respond, asking for more information:

  A: | I've <u>seen</u> it, but I've never <u>eat</u>en there. Is it <u>good</u>?
     | No, I <u>haven't</u>. What's it <u>like</u>?
  B: It's [<u>in</u>teresting]. It's [a Japan<u>ese</u> restaurant], and
     there's [a <u>gar</u>den in it].

► Ask for more specific recommendations:

  A: And [what] should we [<u>order</u>]?
  B: It's probably a good idea to [have the mixed grill],
      because [it's their <u>spec</u>ialty].

► Find out how far, expensive, etc. it is:

  A: | Is it ex<u>pen</u>sive?
     | How ex<u>pen</u>sive is it?
  B: | Not <u>real</u>ly. | [About <u>$</u>15.00 a <u>per</u>son].
     | A <u>lit</u>tle.

5

Find the rule: more present perfect

You have already studied the use of the present perfect with "for" and "since" in Unit 5. Now compare it with a new use.

1 A: How long have you been in Montreal?
  B: I've been here | since June.
                    | for two months.

► What is the verb in the question and answer in the first conversation?
  a) have.
  b) be.
  c) have been.

► What time expressions are used in B's two answers?

► Which time expressions are definite?
  a) since June.
  b) ever.
  c) for two months.

2 A: Have you ever been to Boston?
  B: No, I've never been to the U.S.

► What is the verb in the question and answer in the second conversation?
  a) have.
  b) be.
  c) have been.

► What is the time expression in the second question?
  a) ever.
  b) never.
  And in the answer?
  a) ever.
  b) never.

► Which time expression is indefinite?
  a) for two months.
  b) since June.
  c) ever.

► When do we use the present perfect?
  a) for actions that began in the past and continue until the present.
  b) for actions completed at some indefinite time in the past, or not completed yet.
  c) in both a and b.

Now apply the rule!

Heather is asking Diane some questions. Some of the sentences have mistakes in them. Correct the ones that are wrong.

1 Heather: How long are you a physical therapist?
2 Diane: I started after I finished college, in 1989.
3 Heather: Have you never worked with children?
4 Diane: Yes. In fact I did some training with children before I graduated.
5 Heather: And have you worked with animals, too, when you were studying?
6 Diane: No, I've never worked with animals, only people.

6
Transfer

Ask about someone's experiences, and find out his or her opinion. For example, you can ask about movies, shows or other entertainment. Then change roles and practice again.

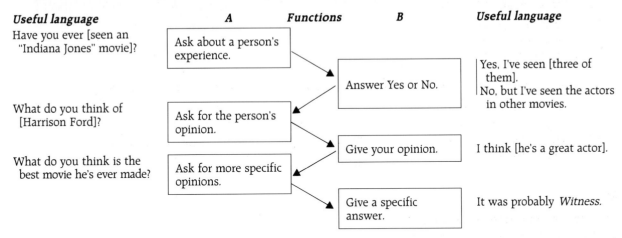

Useful language	A	Functions	B	*Useful language*
Have you ever [seen an "Indiana Jones" movie]?	Ask about a person's experience.		Answer Yes or No.	Yes, I've seen [three of them]. No, but I've seen the actors in other movies.
What do you think of [Harrison Ford]?	Ask for the person's opinion.		Give your opinion.	I think [he's a great actor].
What do you think is the best movie he's ever made?	Ask for more specific opinions.		Give a specific answer.	It was probably *Witness*.

7 🔊
Focus on pronunciation

Many nouns in English are made of more than one part. They are sometimes spelled as one word, sometimes as two. Listen to these noun compounds, and answer the questions:

weekend   dining room
airplane   airplane ticket

▶ What part of the noun compound has the most stress?
   a) the first part.
   b) the second part.

▶ Where is the emphasis in a two-word noun compound?
   a) the stressed syllable of the first word.
   b) the stressed syllable of the second word.

▶ Underline the syllable with the most stress in these noun compounds. Then listen to the tape to confirm your guesses.

   1 travel agency
   2 taxi cabs
   3 tape player
   4 tennis shoes
   5 basketball
   6 basketball game
   7 library card
   8 driver's license
   9 movie theater
   10 hotel reservations

▶ Now rewind the tape and repeat the words.

8
Role play

Do you have any suggestions?

Have you ever seen *Cats*?

Student B: Go to page 73.
Student A: Your friend from another city is visiting you and asks for advice about things to do. Ask about his/her experiences and make suggestions.

JUST LUCK?

Do you have a lucky number? Do you read your horoscope "just for fun"? If the answer is "yes," then chances are good that you are at least a little superstitious.

Numbers are often part of superstitious beliefs. For example, many people think that disasters always occur in threes. In Western cultures, the number 13, especially, is believed to bring bad luck. It is unusual to find a 13th floor in a building. Even psychology professors at a California college complained when their building was numbered 1300 – they were afraid that superstitious students would refuse to take classes there. And on one Friday the 13th, Trans-World Airways found that they had 5% fewer passengers than usual. On the other hand, 8 is supposed to be a lucky number. Princess Beatrice, granddaughter of Queen Elizabeth II of Great Britain, was born on an especially lucky day – August 8, 1988 (8/8/88).

All kinds of people have illogical beliefs about luck. Among actors and actresses, it is considered unlucky to wish someone "good luck" on stage. Instead they say "break a leg." Athletes often have some lucky piece of clothing that they wear to help them win. People who gamble money at horse races or simply play lottery games usually use some personal number to bring them luck: their phone number, car licence number, birthdate, or a number that has come to them in a dream.

Psychologists have an explanation for superstitious beliefs. They say that superstitions are humans' answers to an unpredictable world. The less control we have over something, the more superstitions we will have about it. Believing a superstition makes us feel that things like health, death, love, success and money can be made predictable. Superstitions help reduce stress. And if you're a student taking a test, being calmer will probably help you – even if the reason for your calmness is that you are wearing your "lucky" socks.

Do you think that other people might be superstitious, but not you? Then consider what Alan Dundes, a folklorist from the University of California, Berkeley thinks. He says that our daily lives are full of superstition. "People think that if they take their umbrellas, it won't rain, or if they wash their cars, it will." He also says that advertising couldn't even work without the superstitious magic of "secret" ingredients, and combinations of letters and numbers (usually three) such as "XR3." Dundes claims that half of the weight-loss diets popular at any time work partly because the dieters "believe" they will.

In today's technologically advanced world, we like to think of ourselves as modern, scientific and rational, but Frances Cattermole-Tally, executive editor of the *Encyclopedia of American Popular Beliefs and Superstitions* says that most people really don't think very logically. She defines superstition this way: "I have beliefs. You have superstitions." People will always have superstitions because the basic issues they face every day, like love, death, and health, will always be uncertain.

Read on your own

Warm-up

What is a superstition? All cultures have certain objects or practices that many people believe bring good or bad luck. For example, in the United States, a four-leaf clover is supposed to bring good luck to the person who finds it. Work with one or two other students to list three things that are symbols of good or bad luck in your country.

10
Main ideas

Read the article "Just Luck?" Mark T (true) or F (false) for each of these statements.

1 Unlucky numbers or dates never cause people to change their plans.
2 People often believe that some personal object brings them luck.
3 Superstition is a way to explain events that we cannot control.
4 Advertising presents only logical reasons to encourage people to use a product.
5 Frances Cattermole-Tally says that beliefs and superstitions are the same thing.

11
Focus on words

Find the negative forms of these adjectives in the article, and write them down.

► Do you see a general rule for making adjectives negative? What is it? Which word shows an exception to the rule?

1 usual _____
2 logical _____
3 lucky _____
4 predictable _____
5 certain _____

12
Inferences

Which of these ideas does the article suggest? Mark them with a + (plus); then discuss your answers with a classmate.

1 Superstitions are an important part of culture.
2 It is illogical to read horoscopes and believe in astrology.
3 There is nothing wrong with having superstitious beliefs; it may even help people.
4 Ms. Cattermole-Tally probably thinks that religion is at least partly based on superstition.

13
Making predictions

Work in pairs or small groups to predict what is going to happen in the next month. Are your predictions based on your experience, what you want to believe, or simple guessing? Compare your predictions with other students. Use these topics and any others you think of.

● the weather
● government/elections
● a famous person
● a sports competition

14
Laugh and learn

Look at these cartoons and answer the questions.

> *Vocabulary notes:*
> **hang out** = spend time
> **Beats me** = I don't know
> **earn** = get paid for work

1. HI & LOIS

2. BLONDIE

▶ In the Blondie cartoon, one woman says "My husband's." What does this mean?
  a) something her husband has.
  b) she has more than one husband.
  c) her husband is.

▶ In the Hi & Lois cartoon, one woman says "my husband's." What does this mean?
  a) something her husband has.
  b) she has more than one husband.
  c) her husband is.

▶ In which cartoon could you change "my husband's" to "his"?
  a) Hi & Lois.
  b) Blondie.

Now apply the rule

Review what you know. Fill in the chart with the correct forms. Then complete Jean's letter to her sister.

possessive noun	*possessive adjective*	*possessive pronoun*
boy's/man's	....	his
girl's/woman's	her	....
....	their	....
X	....	mine
X	your	....
X	....	ours

Dear Pia,
  I just got _____ letter today. Tell Mom not to worry. And tell her I *have* tried to call her. You know how much she talks on the phone. _____'s line is always busy. But _____ isn't - she can call Heather and me sometimes, too.
  Heather is fine. She is doing well in _____ French classes. She still has an accent, of course, but _____ is worse (My French sounds more like Italian!)
  You asked about my housemates. _____ names are Marta and Diane. They are almost like aunts to Heather. We all have _____ own rooms, and keep them clean (except for Heather - _____ is a disaster area).
  I'm really enjoying myself here. I'm learning a lot in _____ courses at the WHF Institute. And I've met lots of interesting people. Anyway, it has been a great summer for me - I hope _____ is just as good!
  See you soon,
    Jean

15 ⇄ 📼
Live from CWHF

In this program Marie Dubonnet tells us about what there is to do in Montreal from August 16th to August 23rd.

Marie Dubonnet will give the details of these events:

- "The Comedy Nest" – comedy act
- The Latin Quarter Walk-a-thon
- Montreal Film Festival
- Montreal Mondial World Triathlon
- St. Jean sur le Richelieu Hot-air Balloon Festival
- *Shear Madness* – play

Before you listen, choose two events that seem the most interesting to you.
The first time you listen, wait for Marie to announce the events you selected, and write down as many details as you can about them.

Find other students who chose one or both of the same events as you did. Share the information you wrote down with these students.

Listen again to check the details, and add any other information you missed the first time.

► Do the events you selected still seem interesting to you? Ask classmates to give the details of some of the events that you did not make notes for.

► Pretend that you are substituting for Marie Dubonnet. Using your notes, announce one of the events to your group. Or make up a radio announcement of some event you know about.

Student B

8 Role play *(page 69)*

Student B: You are visiting the city where Student A lives, and you want some recommendations of things to do. Choose some of these to ask about:

tourist attractions	museums	parks
discos/nightclubs	theater/plays	sports
eating out	buying souvenirs	special events

Grammar review game:
Grammar streets

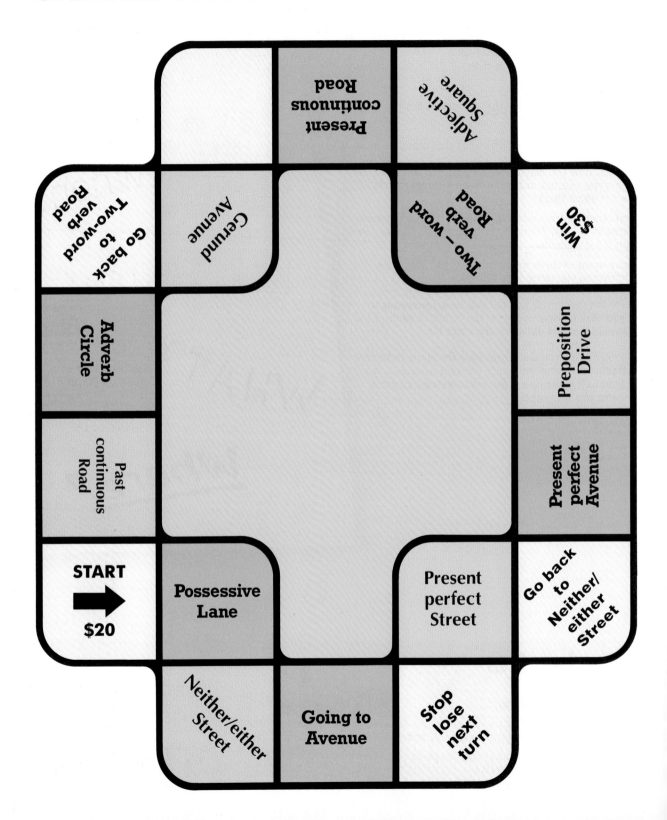

Present continuous Road

Adjective Square

Go back to Two-word verb Road

Gerund Avenue

Two-word verb Road

Win $30

Adverb Circle

Preposition Drive

Past continuous Road

Present perfect Avenue

START

$20

Possessive Lane

Present perfect Street

Go back to Neither/either Street

Neither/either Street

Going to Avenue

Stop lose next turn

Student A

Going to:

What you going to do tomorrow?
Tex and Kenji are going to go to the park to run.
Yves going to call Jean from the office.

Present Continuous:

Is Heather liking her French class?
Please repeat. I'm not understanding.
Yves can't have lunch now; he talks with a client.

Present Perfect (Red):

Marta has never visit New York.
Who you have talked to today?
Did Diane ever used chopsticks before?

Two-word verb:

Heather is at a friend's house. Jean is going to pick up her later.
Yves felt warm, so he took it off his tie.
How do you turn on the tape player on?

Possessive:

Tex wants you to call him up. Her number is 672-3498.
I don't have a blue umbrella. Is it your?
Where can Diane get a pen? She's has run out of ink.

Adverb:

Please talk quiet in the library.
The Concorde plane flies very fast.
Kenji always writes careful in English.

Rules:

This is a game for two players, A is Red and B is Blue. Student A has the red spaces on the game board and uses the red part of this page. Student B has the blue spaces on the game board and uses the blue part of this page.

▶ Each player begins with $100. A player gets $20 every time he/she passes START.

▶ Toss a coin. If it is heads, move ahead two spaces; if Tails, move only one space.

▶ When a player lands on his/her colored space (red lands on red, blue lands on blue) nothing happens.

▶ When a player lands on a yellow space, he/she must do what the space says.

▶ When a player lands on the other player's colored space (blue lands on a red space, or red lands on a blue space), he/she must listen to a sentence from a list for that space, and correct it if it is wrong.

▶ When a player makes a mistake in correcting a sentence, he/she must pay a $10 parking fine. Players keep a total of all the money they have, subtracting fines and adding any money they get.

▶ The game ends when one player runs out of money or when the teacher says to stop. The player with the most money wins.

Past Continuous:

It was raining when I was arriving at class.
Tex's alarm clock was ringing at exactly 6:00 A.M.
I read a book when suddenly the lights went out.

Gerund:

What do you enjoy to do in your free time?
Diane keeps exercising even when she's not at home.
Marta misses go to the beach in Brazil.

Adjective:

Marie Dubonnet is the better radio reporter in Montreal.
Who is more tall, Yves or Tex?
Heather is youngest person in her family.

Preposition:

Our neighbors live in the apartment next to ours.
Jean likes to park her car front her building.
Tex likes to sit in the floor to study.

Present Perfect (Blue):

Kenji was a medical student for five years.
Yves lives in Montreal since he was a baby.
We have studied English last year.

Neither/Either:

Kenji can't speak French, and either can Tex.
My father's not tall, but he's not short neither.
Diane isn't married and Marta isn't either.

Student B

Optional extras Units 5–8

Whenever you have extra time . . .

1 Find someone who . . . *(Unit 5)*

Talk with other people in your class and find someone who . . .

Have you studied another foreign language?

No I haven't. I've only studied English.

1 . . . has studied another foreign language (besides English).
2 . . . has lived in this city or town since he/she was a child.
3 . . . has flown in a helicopter.
4 . . . has not used a microcomputer.
5 . . . has lived in this city or town for less than five years.
6 . . . has visited at least three foreign countries.
7 . . . has not watched television for two days or more.
8 . . . has been to the dentist since his/her birthday.
9 . . . has not missed a class since the beginning of the term.
10 . . . has known the teacher for more than a year.

2 Tic-tac-toe *(Unit 5)*

Talk about things you have done. Student A is X; Student B is O. Student A chooses a square and asks Student B a question using the present perfect. If the question is correct, he/she marks an X. Student B answers in a complete sentence. If Student B's answer is correct, he/she asks the next question.

since	how long	lived
last year	wanted	a long time
studied	worked	for

3 Verb search *(Unit 6)*

There are eight verbs in this puzzle that are followed by gerunds when they are used in sentences. Work with a partner and find them all as fast as you can. Try to be the fastest in the class.

R	E	Q	A	A	S	D	W
E	B	U	E	E	K	I	A
M	M	I	S	S	E	S	N
E	A	T	V	T	E	L	T
M	I	N	D	U	P	I	F
B	L	Z	E	D	O	K	V
E	N	J	O	Y	F	E	X
R	O	F	I	N	I	S	H

4 Share information *(Unit 6)*

Student B: Go to page 78.
Student A: Read this description of Anne Susan Vandenberg. Student B knows some things about her twin sister, Maria Susana. Find out how the sisters are alike by using NEGATIVE sentences to talk about them. Find as many negative similarities as you can.

Useful language

A: Anne Susan's friends and family don't call her by her first name. They call her Sue.
B: People don't call Maria Susana by her first name either. They also call her Sue.

This is Anne Susan Vandenberg, but her friends and family call her Sue. She was born in New York City. Her mother died when she was born and she was adopted by the Vandenberg family. She lived in Chicago, Illinois until she went to college. Then she moved to Atlanta, Georgia. In college her first major was history, but later she decided to study journalism instead.

Now she works as a reporter. She travels a lot because of her job, so she gave up her other job singing with a jazz band. She doesn't have time to practice. When she can, she plays tennis, but not very often. She should get more exercise. She loves all kinds of movies, except violent ones like police movies and westerns. Her favorite actor is Charlie Chaplin.

5 Rhythm practice (Unit 7)

Repeat each line. Then practice as Group A and Group B.

A   Serious Problems   B

There's really something funny
About Mary Lou.

    She never seems to know
    What she wants to do.

She picks up a book
Then puts it down.

    She makes her hair blond
    Then dyes it brown.
She writes a long letter
Then tears it up.

    She even forgets to feed
    Her little pup.

She calls up her friends
Then wonders why.

    She just says hello
    Then says goodbye.

Her mind must be floating
Like the clouds above.

    Don't you see? That's the answer!
    She must be in love!

6 What do you see? (Unit 7)

Student B: Go to page 78.
Student A: Imagine you are on a beautiful, sandy beach. The sun is shining. You are on one of the islands in Hawaii. Describe the sensations you experience so that Student B can guess where you are. Talk about what you see, hear, smell, feel, and also *how* you feel. But don't say what you are actually doing or where you are.

Then listen to Student B talk about his/her sensations. Try to guess where he/she is. Ask questions like these:

What do you see around you?
Can you hear any noises?

7 The day after (Unit 7)

Work with a partner to decide what you are going to do to clean up this room after last night's birthday celebration. Make a list and then discuss it with another pair of students.

8 Time travel role play
(Unit 8)

Student B: Go to page 78.
Student A: Imagine you have traveled to the next century in a time machine. Ask Student B (a citizen of the future world) to explain how things have changed compared to the "past" world you come from. Find out about:

- telephones and communications
- cars and transportation
- work and study schedules
- houses
- money

Useful language

How have schools changed?
Have telephones changed much?

78

Optional Extras   Units 5–8
Student B

4 Share information *(page 76)*

Read this description of Maria Susana Martinez. Student A knows some things about her twin sister, Anne Susan. Find out how the sisters are alike by using NEGATIVE sentences to talk about them. Find as many negative similarities as you can.

> **Useful language**
>
> B: Most people don't call Maria Susana by her first name. They call her Sue.
> A: Neither do Anne Susan's friends and family. They call her Sue.

This is Maria Susana Martinez. But most people call her Sue. She was born in New York City. Her mother died when she was born and she was adopted by the Martinez family. She grew up in San Diego, California and went to live in Philadelphia, Pennsylvania after she finished college. In college she began to study English, but she changed her major to political science. Now she teaches history in a high-school in Philadelphia. When she was still studying, she played piano with a jazz band, but she stopped. She's too busy now to practice. She goes jogging on days she doesn't have to teach, but she doesn't run in the winter or when it's raining. She probably needs more

exercise. She loves old movies, but she hates westerns. Her favorite actor is Charlie Chaplin.

6 What do you see? *(page 77)*

Student A is trying to imagine what it feels like to be in a certain place. Listen to Student A talk about his/her sensations. Try to guess where he/she is. Ask questions like these:

What do you see around you?
Can you hear any noises?

Now imagine you are in the lounge of a ski resort in Aspen, Colorado during the winter. A fire is burning in the fireplace. . .

Describe the sensations you experience so that Student A can guess where you are. Talk about what you see, hear, smell, feel, and also *how* you feel. But don't say what you are actually doing or where you are.

8 Time travel role play *(page 77)*

Imagine you are a citizen of the next century. You are the official guide for all visitors from the past. Student A is visiting, and has a lot of questions. Here is some information which will help you.

> **Useful language**
>
> Schools haven't changed at all.
> We haven't used telephones for 50 years. Now we use image-phones.

* telephones: image-phones for many years. Latest thing is a kind of phone that you think into, not talk into. Invented five years ago.

* cars and transportation: cars not used. People travel by hover-jets that float on air.

* work and study schedules: school is the same, but work is two days a week for twelve hours. Two more days are for training.

* houses: all modern houses are one big space that is divided by laser beams that make walls and furniture.

* money: money stopped being used 35 years ago. Now people just talk to their pocket computers.